HONESTLY

GETTING REAL ABOUT JESUS AND OUR MESSY LIVES

DANIEL FUSCO
with D. R. JACOBSEN

NAVPRESS

A NavPress resource published in alliance
with Tyndale House Publishers, Inc.

NavPress is the publishing ministry of The Navigators, an international Christian organization and leader in personal spiritual development. NavPress is committed to helping people grow spiritually and enjoy lives of meaning and hope through personal and group resources that are biblically rooted, culturally relevant, and highly practical.

For more information, visit www.NavPress.com.

PRAISE FOR
DANIEL FUSCO'S *HONESTLY*

Raw and real. Those are the words I would use to describe Daniel Fusco's book *Honestly*. No matter what you're dealing with, *Honestly* shows how God wants to do new things in and through you. I so appreciate Daniel—his passion, joy, and commitment to the gospel. It's evident in this book.

KEVIN PALAU
Author of *Unlikely*

Sometimes when I am fast-forwarding through a commercial break while watching a TV show that's recorded on my DVR, something catches my eye that makes me stop, rewind, and actually watch an ad or a movie trailer. That is how I see this book by my friend Daniel Fusco: In a sea of regularly scheduled static, the words on these pages are disruptive and worth pausing for. He is willing to "go there," and you will be glad to let him take you—not to merely pay lip service to the great ache of our hearts or to put a Band-Aid on a bullet hole, but because acknowledging the elephant in the room that is our messiness allows Jesus to deal with it. This is a book that needed to be written, needs to be read, and must be allowed to read you—honestly.

LEVI LUSKO
Pastor of Fresh Life Church, Montana, and author of *Through the Eyes of a Lion*

Daniel Fusco is a breath of fresh air in a stale room; he gives us what we all need to survive this side of resurrection—not trite, formulaic answers, but *honesty*. His raw, candid transparency is great, and mixed with his hopeful love of life, it's a beautiful read.

JOHN MARK COMER
Pastor for teaching and vision at Bridgetown: A Jesus Church, and author of *Loveology* and *Garden City*

Daniel Fusco is an incredible friend and an amazing pastor. *Honestly* is a great title for his book because it perfectly describes who Daniel is: He's the real deal. We live in a world that has been broken by sin. As a result, life gets messy—sometimes even downright nasty. Daniel does a great job helping Christians develop a theology that informs them Jesus is not only greater than the mess and nastiness that life can bring, but He can also use that mess to make you into a masterpiece. Every person who follows Jesus will be encouraged and challenged by reading *Honestly*.

PAT HOOD
Pastor of LifePoint Church in Smyrna, Tennessee, and author of *The Sending Church*

Daniel Fusco takes dead aim on cliché Christianity, without creating any of the collateral damage of cynicism that so often accompanies our well-intentioned attempts to challenge an unexamined faith. *Honestly* is honest, humorous, and always challenging. I recommend it.

LARRY OSBORNE
Author and pastor, North Coast Church, California

Do you long to understand the trials and messiness in your life? If so, you'll want to read *Honestly* by Daniel Fusco. He gets real by unpacking biblical truths to help our messy lives make sense, and how God can use our messes to bless others. This is a must read.

DAVE FERGUSON
Lead pastor of Community Christian Church, Chicago, and lead visionary of NewThing

I started my Christian walk in the midst of a terrible mess! I had just lost my father. As a result we had lost the family business, and we were falling into serious poverty. It was one of the darkest times of my life, and I was only twelve years old. Yet Jesus' resurrection power was so real to me and my family in the middle of it all. Having experienced God's transforming power in the midst of those hard times, I can say "Yes!" and "Amen!" to Daniel Fusco's wonderful new book, *Honestly*.

LUIS PALAU
World evangelist, author of *Out of the Desert*

I love how real and authentic Daniel is. His heart is so open and his way of communicating is totally disarming, all the while addressing profound and necessary spiritual truths and encouraging you to dive deeper and deeper into Jesus.

JEREMY CAMP
Songwriter and recording artist

To Lynn, Obadiah, Maranatha, and Annabelle.

Words cannot express my love.

Let's keep enjoying our messy life together with Jesus!

CONTENTS

SHOUT OUTS

TO MY FAMILY:

I wouldn't be who I am today without you. To all the Fuscos and Cappadonas and the other six thousand relatives in my extended family, thank you for your overwhelming love and large personalities. Grandpa, Grandma, Dad, Trisha, and Jodi, I am grateful for each one of you. You mean so much to me. Plus we are blessed with Marianne, Jim, Hal, and all the kids! Our family is amazing! And Lynn, Obadiah, Maranatha, and Annabelle, next to Jesus you are the best thing that has ever happened to me. You have my whole heart, always.

TO MY WRITING TEAM:

I feel so blessed that God has put together this team. To Jenni Burke of D. C. Jacobson & Associates, thank you for believing in me and taking this journey with me. Your wisdom and tenacity are a gift. To David Jacobsen, you have taught me much on this journey. Thank you for partnering your heart and skills to coauthor this book with me. To Caitlyn Carlson, thank you for how much you have invested in this book and in me. Your belief and expertise have meant the world. To Don Pape, words cannot express how grateful I am for you. We are here right now because of you. Thank you for believing in me! And to the entire NavPress/Tyndale team, thank you for using your gifts as part of this project and every project. You are advancing God's Kingdom through the work you do.

TO MY CHURCH FAMILY:

I am eternally grateful to belong to such an amazing family of faith. Crossroads is an extraordinary community, and I am humbled and blessed to be a part of it. Let's keep simply responding to Jesus together to transform our community and our world. To the Servant Leadership Team, Executive Team, pastors/directors, and staff, thank you for being "all-in" on the work that God has entrusted to us. Your servant's hearts and joy inspire me.

TO MY GOD:

Thank you, Lord, for giving me an abundant life in Christ. Thank you for loving me even when I am unlovable. Thank you for the empowering of your Spirit for the work of ministry. Thank you for your grace and forgiveness. And for the mess—amen!

START HERE

I looked up from the magazine I was reading. John Coltrane's *A Love Supreme* was still blaring from the stereo. Dad was framed in the doorway of my bedroom, one hand in the pocket of his jeans. The hall light glinted on the top of his head.

"Hey, how's Mom?"

They'd been away all day, the two of them, visiting the doctor. Now that I thought about it, all day was too long for a trip to the doctor. Hadn't they left right after breakfast? I thought so. My sisters and I had stayed at the table, drinking a fresh pot of coffee, enjoying the feel of summertime freedom and swapping stories about our just-finished college semesters. What had I done the rest of the day, and why hadn't I paid attention to how long Mom and Dad had been gone?

I noticed my father's hand trembling, and he reached up and gripped the doorframe. The digital numbers on my bedside table read 9:13.

"Danny," he began. "Danny. She . . ."

He looked like he was trying to swallow something. My

magazine tipped out of my hands and slid off the bed and onto the carpet. Dad's hand white-knuckled the door frame.

"Dad, what's—"

"Your mom has cancer."

How had I crossed the room without moving? Dad's body seemed to slide down the door frame in slow motion. My father never cried, but he was crying now. And me beside him. His mustache and beard were thick with it, and his shoulders shook with it. With fear. We sat crumpled on the floor, and I held on to him, as we tried to hold on to hope. The sound of our sobbing became a metronome, counting out the seconds and then the terrible minutes of our new and terribly changed life—a life that only happened to *other* families.

Two years passed. Sometimes raced, sometimes crawled. Four semesters of college and chemo and radiation and Christmas Eves where we stuffed ourselves silly and pretended we were as happy as we'd always been.

Mom's brain lesions metastasized: lungs, bones, the rest of her brain. I shaved off my first head of dreadlocks to stand in solidarity with Mom and her new peach-fuzz look. Mom even got a wig and quipped, "I had to get cancer so I could be a fun blonde!" But honestly, we were trying to believe the best, even though we knew the worst was probably coming.

I was getting ready for my final year at New Jersey's Rutgers University. My twin sister, Jodi, would also be graduating from Rutgers and heading off to law school, while our older sister, Trisha, was finishing her master's degree in vocal performance for opera. My grandparents, Anita and Anthony, lived with us to help care for Mom as my father continued to work. We spent a ton of time at home, especially after Mom came home from the hospital the final time to be on hospice. Our house was packed with people: aunts, uncles, cousins, nieces, nephews, siblings, parents, and friends who were as close as family. We Fuscos did family right. Thick and thin, ups and downs, we were a *clan*, you know? Freakin' *smothered* in love. Wasn't nothing we couldn't fix with a meal, with wine, with talking late into the night, with laughter so loud it felt like it was inside your heart.

At least that's what we'd thought.

When Mom took her last breath—when Dad lay down beside her on the rented hospital bed and just shook like a leaf—I remember thinking . . . nothing. Absolutely nothing. Because it didn't compute. There was no category for this. If life was a well-lit room, then Mom dying was a power outage. Everything in my life went dark, and there was nothing to do but wait for the electricity to come back on.

Even though I knew the light *wouldn't* come back on, I waited anyway. Because what else could a boy do?

. . .

We all have these types of stories, don't we? For each one of us, there are certain things that just don't make any sense. You just look at your life, you look at your circumstances, you compare your life to others, and you think to yourself,

That's not what life's supposed to be about. That's not what's meant to happen.

The details are different, but life's equally messy for all of us.

I'm not talking about only the gut-punch stuff, either. As a college kid, I had to deal with my mom dying of cancer. That's an appalling example of life's messiness. But life's messiness isn't just the negative headlines—it's everything that keeps us unbalanced. Life is extraordinarily unpredictable. Things happen that we can't fathom—some of which we choose, and some of which are chosen for us. Changing jobs, dating and breaking up, moving, and having kids, all the way down to getting an awkward text from a friend or forgetting we're out of milk (or money).

Messiness is a universal concept, and the church in Ephesus in the mid-first century had its fair share. The apostle Paul had started the church there, and as he traveled and started other congregations, he kept a close eye on the established churches. Because travel took so long in those days, and he couldn't be everywhere at once, he had to write the churches letters to help them keep focused in the midst of life. The letter he wrote to the Ephesians was not precipitated by extraordinary circumstances, either—it was just normal life happening in Ephesus.

But they, like us, needed simple encouragement and direction.

Messiness describes the things we find ourselves dealing with on a daily, weekly, monthly, and even lifelong basis.

Things happen that don't seem to make much sense, and then they keep right on happening.

Here's the thing. Maybe you've been told that if you're a good Christian, everything will be sunshine and rainbows. Or that good things happen to good people and bad things happen to bad people. Perhaps a pastor or a parent has let you know, directly or by implication, that your messy life is no one's fault but your own. Maybe you've always lived around people who've told you—or you've even told yourself—that life *isn't* messy . . . and so anything messy just gets swept under the rug and ignored.

Or like so many others, you've chosen to flee "organized religion" because the pat answers, clichés, and lack of authenticity didn't jibe with the more mysterious and unpredictable parts of life. Maybe you asked the honest questions, only to be chastised or brushed aside.

Told you were sinning, even.

But you've got to know this: The Christian message is *not* that life isn't messy.

Honestly, it's the opposite. The Christian message doesn't claim that life is neat or tidy or straightforward. The Christian message says that life is—and always will be—exceedingly, frustratingly messy. You know it, and so do I.

So I promise you: Nothing I write in this book will contradict the root truth that life doesn't always make sense.

But there's another part to the message. It's just as true, and even more important.

Yes, life is messy.

And Jesus is real.

That's a big deal. That's the gospel. That word *gospel,* which is a churchy word for sure, means *good news.* And the fact that Jesus is real in the midst of life's messiness *is* good news. He's where everything that's healing and good and grace-filled begins and ends.

. . .

I met my friend Ilya in high school. He's a *nasty* drummer, while I play both the electric and upright bass. Together we formed a band called . . . Choda. (Don't ask.) Even though we went away to different colleges, our friendship remained strong and music connected us. While we were apart, we'd spend all our free time practicing our instruments, and all our free cash buying new albums. Then whenever we were back together on the weekends, we'd always play *grab bag.*

That meant we'd sit around, sometimes all night long, and play DJ for each other, sharing the music that we had been digging. I'd slot in a disc, find my favorite track, and we'd listen in silence. When the track ended, it was his turn to pick. Back and forth, for hours on end, song after song, group after group. Occasionally we'd hit pause if we needed to digest something super meaty, or we'd track back to hear a particular riff a third or a tenth time.

A lot of times we'd talk about the songs, analyzing what we were hearing, but other times we were silent. Enrapt. Our faces told the story, even if our voices didn't. I'd see his forehead scrunch up as he tried to process a brutally amazing rhythmic syncopation, or I could feel my eyes bugging out when the band would extend the harmonic palette.

Then we'd hit the grease trucks for some late-night or early-morning eats![1]

Ilya and I decided one night that we were going to listen to Coltrane's *A Love Supreme* in its entirety. That was a rarity for grab-bag nights, but it was an album that deserved it. Plus the album was designed in four movements—Acknowledgement, Resolution, Pursuance, Psalm—and we wanted to hear the entire arc of the music, in our hearts, in one sitting. So we stationed ourselves on my hardwood floor, each leaning back against a chair. There was a reason we chose the floor over the chairs: We wanted to be *right* in front of my speakers. I had a sick stereo, including speakers the size of Jabba the Hutt. I twisted the volume knob, hit the play button, and settled back onto the floor, and a second later the eloquent sound of Trane's classic quartet embraced us.

We didn't talk. *A Love Supreme* did all the speaking, and it spoke straight to our souls. I closed my eyes, to better hear the sounds pouring from the speakers. There were the shimmering cymbals of Elvin Jones, the hypnotic thump of Jimmy Garrison's bass, and the landscape of colors painted by McCoy Tyner's piano. Over it all came John Coltrane on the tenor sax, by turns authoritative and plaintive. Single notes seemed to stretch on and on, carrying me with them

---

[1] After college, Ilya and I stuffed my minivan and a trailer full of our instruments, some clothes, and literally thousands of compact discs, and moved across the country to seek our musical fame and fortune. We ended up in Ashland, Oregon, before moving to the San Francisco Bay Area, and we . . . well, that's actually a tale that will have to wait for my next book. But trust me, two Jersey boys loose on the highways of America was the start of some killer stories!

like a tightrope across a chasm, only to morph into one of his patented sheets of sound that threatened to melt my face off.

It was beautiful, yes, but it went beyond beauty. It was *real*. It was tapping into something inside my soul that words couldn't reach, or at least at that point in my life *hadn't* reached. It was necessary and urgent and sad and messy and hopeful and honest.

And it was love.

Love incarnated in the body of songs, movements, solos and runs, and group explorations. A Love Supreme. Thirty-five minutes and forty-three seconds passed in a moment. Eternity had touched time, and we were there to witness it. To participate in it. With wide-open hearts.

Ilya and I sat frozen, silent, basking in the afterglow. It almost seemed the sudden silence in the room was bowing down to the sounds that had just filled it.

At last we managed to capture with words the feelings that were cascading like waterfalls through our souls.

"Oh man . . ."

"Whoa . . ."

Both of us were changed. For real, forever. We had gone under the waters of baptism, beneath the water of Trane's offering, and we had ascended with fresh vision. There was simply no way we could remain as we'd been. We were born again. And we knew—*knew*, in our bones and the depths of our being, without a doubt—that we'd devote our lives to figuring out how to make music like Trane had made. Not to be famous like him, not to copy him, not to just understand music, but because we wanted to change people's lives with *our* music like he'd changed us with his.

We wanted to make music that moved the soul.

We wanted to create light that would shine in the darkness.

We wanted to gift beauty to a world that was all too often ugly.

Did we?

Yes—absolutely yes.

And no. No way, no how.

See, it's complicated. Yes, we created—and still create—music. And that music moves the soul and shines in the darkness and adds beauty to the world. But also . . . no. How could music really do all that? Can music feed the hungry and clothe the naked? Can music really fix what is perpetually broken?

Point is, *nothing* we do is completely free of the mess. Even the greatest works of art are messy. And to many listeners, certain kinds of jazz sound like they're *all* mess![2]

Which is why life is a lot like jazz: one giant mess.

At least to the untrained ear.

But when we listen closely to life, we can start to hear the melodies in the midst of the mess. It takes study, and digging deep, and being patient enough to learn. And if we're lucky, or blessed, we discover something about the mess: Nothing *we* do is free of the mess, but sometimes in our mess we catch the tune of the Master.

---

[2] If we're talking about some of the jazz *I* like to play, and we're talking about my wife listening, then she'd be like, "Amen to the mess comment!"

Because here's the thing: Jesus really *did* feed the hungry and clothe the naked. He fixed what is perpetually broken. He can still do that today! But he does it by standing in the middle of the mess, holding that bass line and weaving together a song out of the cacophony of human life exploding all around him.

Life will always be messy. But Jesus will always be our beauty in the middle of the mess. Jesus is our Love Supreme.

. . .

When you're listening to a great jazz musician, you don't feel excited and satisfied when the song is over.

Like, no one goes, "Yes, I got from the start of the song to the end of the song!" In fact, when the final note fades, you're actually bummed. Because Trane, as he was affectionately called, took you on a journey and, in the process, revealed to you amazing, beautiful, and unexpected things. You would never have guessed from the beginning of the song, or even the middle of the song, where you would end up. Why? Because you experienced the process of improvisation.

It's been said that humans love the outcome, while God loves the process. (Therefore, God must love jazz, right?) And I want *Honestly* to be about experiencing the process.

Of living a messy life, and living it alongside Jesus.

Even improvised jazz tends to be highly structured. Yet no one *notices* the structure because the structure is not as important as the experience. The structure is there to serve the experience, not the other way around.

So this book? It's a lot like a piece of improvised music. All of *Honestly* is based on Paul's letter to the Ephesians. Back in 2014, I had a blast walking through Ephesians with my church family at Crossroads, and over the course of eleven weeks, we looked at every verse of that great letter! And God did some extraordinary things in our church family and community during that series.[3]

But when it came time to put fingers to keyboard, so to speak, I wanted to do something different from "cleaning up" my sermons and putting them in a book.

I wanted to improvise.

Like at a jazz gig (but with a lot less sweat), I wanted to improvise on the stunning themes of Paul's letter: the messiness of life, the crazy good news of Jesus, what we do about the mess as we relate to each other, and how we relate to God—*and* how God's love reigns supreme over and through all of it. I wanted to *explore*, and just like jazz players take their initial cues from a "lead sheet," I wanted Ephesians to be the lead sheet for this book.

Each chapter of this book has its own special truth bomb, waiting to explode in someone's heart and mind. The chapter that hits *you* will probably be different from the chapter that hits your friend. I'll be much happier if you *experience* this book rather than if you *finish* it. I would be overjoyed if, in

---

[3] If you're an "every verse in order" kind of person, you can give this book to someone else, and then listen to the entire sermon series called "Life Is Messy" at www.crossroadschurch.net.

some way, this book helps you see the beauty of Jesus in the midst of your messy life. And my joy would overflow if you experience Jesus in fresh ways on your life's journey.

Before we start, here's my promise to you: I promise to be honest. As honest as I can be, on every page. Because life's too short for anything else.

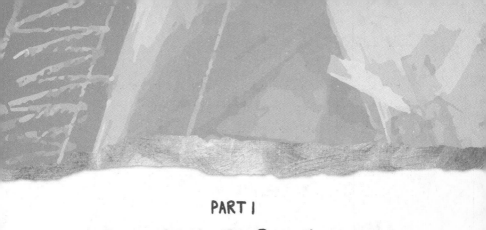

PART I

ACKNOWLEDGEMENT

ACKNOWLEDGE THE MESS

I, Paul, am under God's plan as an apostle, a special agent
of Christ Jesus, writing to you faithful believers.

EPHESIANS 1:1

So here we are, in the middle of the mess.

Maybe you've lost your job. Or hate your job. Maybe your best friend abandoned you, or you've never had a best friend. Maybe you're pulling out your hair because your teenager is doing stupid stuff and you can't get him to realize it's stupid. Maybe your closest relationships are strained. Or worse, boring. Maybe you feel betrayed by your body or your parents or your church. Whatever the specifics, we all have stuff in our lives that seems to make zero sense. Things that hurt us or confuse us or make us doubt we'll ever be able to catch our breath.

That messiness goes along with being human. All of us were born as broken people into broken families living in a broken world. Life happens amid that rubble.

What a fun place to start a book, in the middle of the mess! But since I promised to be honest, we've got to start with what's wrong. We have to acknowledge that everything is not okay. That it's actually *less* than okay, a *lot* of the time.

Trouble is, like we talked about earlier, the Christian message sometimes gets hijacked. Ever been told that if you're really tuned-in to God, your life won't be messy? That everything will work out? Like the messiness is all pre-Jesus, and after you get saved life will always come up roses. But the honest truth is, that stuff isn't true.

Just remember, no matter how deep into the mess we get in this first part of the book, the message doesn't stop there. Good news is coming. Messiness, by itself, is not good news! But messiness that Jesus can work in and through? Absolutely good news!

You may not believe me. And you don't have to. But I bet at least part of you believes that, or wants to believe it, which is why you're reading this book. Because you're looking for someone to shoot straight with you about how messy and unpredictable life is. And I know firsthand. I'm a starter for team Life Is Messy.

If you're hurting today, or confused, or just plain tired, you've come to the right place. Remember that I'm right there with you. We're going to walk into this together. And not so we can have a pity party or rant about how unfair life is. We're after something bigger and far better. We're chasing something that's a mix of joy and wholeness and grace and peace. We're after something that's part contentment and part purpose.

And we're going to do it together, starting with acknowledgement. Life *is* messy, period.

After all, if life wasn't messy—if we could find peace on our own, without Jesus—the book of Ephesians wouldn't exist. (Or the whole rest of the Bible!) Paul never uses the words *life is messy* in his letter to the Ephesians, but he talks an awful lot about how God speaks healing into the messy parts of our lives. Why not take the next twenty or so minutes, grab your Bible, and read through the entire letter. You'll see it clear as day.

So as we crack open the good news in Ephesians, we're going to discover that we aren't the first people, or even the billion-and-first people, to struggle with the messiness of life. Which means we have a lot to learn from Paul about how to live in the midst of it all.

Again, you're not alone. I'm right here with you in the messiness, and so is every other person who's ever lived.

Including Jesus, too, as we're about to discover.

RIFFING ON THE MESS
- What mess are you in?

1.2

PERCEPTIONS AND PRESENCE

*Because of the sacrifice of the Messiah, his blood
poured out on the altar of the Cross.*

EPHESIANS 1:7

I was watching this TV drama the other night, and I had to laugh. The premise wasn't *quite* as unbelievable as one of those Lifetime heartstring-tuggers, but it was close.

The show was about an unmarried teen mom and her

son. There's a stepdad in the picture, but that doesn't stop the kid from almost getting killed and later from running away. His family doesn't really understand him, and the son doesn't help things by refusing to take over the family business. Instead he becomes a nomad, wandering from town to town with no real job. His family tries to help, but they throw up their hands when he starts getting political and religious—two things that are off limits in a lot of families. All too soon, he gets in way over his head and ends up on the wrong side of some powerful enemies. He's slandered, tortured, and killed. What a downer.

Okay, I've gotta stop before too many of you catch on. If I told you that the kid, after a commercial break, resurrected from the dead, you'd be like, "C'mon, Fusco, we see what you did there. You're talking about Jesus, not a Lifetime movie."

Guilty.

But you have to admit, I didn't need to change anything in the summary of Jesus' life. He really did have one of the messiest lives you can imagine. Think about the sheer emotional stress that threatened to overwhelm him every day. Powerful religious and political leaders trying to trap and destroy him, a family that didn't quite get who he was and what he was about, friends questioning and exasperating and betraying him, strangers demanding his time and energy.[1]

So there's no better teacher than Jesus when it comes to dealing with the messiness of life. He's lived the messiness,

---

[1] You know how he dealt with all that? Prayer. Lots and lots of prayer. Feel free to skip ahead to page 85 if you want to learn more about that.

and he's come out the other side. And the life of Jesus testifies to a key truth: God loves to bring blessings out of perceived cursings.

Let me say that again. God loves to bring blessings out of *perceived* cursings. I highlight the word *perceived* because certain messy circumstances only *seem* to be one thing, when really they are *another* thing, or *more* than one thing.

Maybe a better way to say it would be that something can start out as a curse, but it doesn't have to remain one.

I say that with humility. If someone had told me, back when I was twenty, that my mom dying of cancer only *seemed* to be a tragedy, it would have been a race to see whether I would cuss out or knock out that person.

So I'm going to be very careful as we explore this idea, and you have the right to cuss me out or toss the book across the room. In no way is it my desire to minimize or objectify the wounds created by life's messiness. I know that scars are real, and often raw. Even trying to address them is fraught with danger.

But honestly? Deep down we all desire to integrate our pain into our lives in a way that makes us healthy, happy, and hopeful. And the only reason I'm trying this in the first place is because I care—so, props for trying, at least?

Here's where we might see a ray of hope. Issues precede miracles. Think about that. Nothing miraculous has ever happened to someone that didn't first begin with an issue that needed to be fixed or transformed. I have personal issues, health issues, work issues, and existential issues. So do you!

You can't be a human being and not have issues. But it's inside these issues—this messiness—that we can see God's creative and transformative intervention.

Brothers and sisters, if you have issues, you are a *prime* candidate for God to do something miraculous. Issues are God's opportunities.

You don't have to trust me yet. At least don't judge me yet! This *is* tough. Every single week I hear about folks who are struggling with the messiness of life, and I'm like, "Lord, do we *have* to have these issues? Can't you just do your work without there being a calamity or a difficulty first?"

I don't know you, but I do know my own life. Looking back at my mom's cancer, I can say that God didn't *have* to allow that to happen. *But* what God has done since then, in and through that horrible circumstance—and it *was* horrible—is absolutely, breathtakingly, unexpectedly good. Not just in my life, but in the lives of countless others. Jesus is with me—has been and will be with me—in the midst of my messiness.

God is God, even in the mess. *Especially* in the mess. Even when we don't get what he's doing.

RIFFING ON PERCEPTION AND PRESENCE

- What does it mean for *your* life that Jesus dealt with the same kind of messiness as every human?
- Be honest: How does the idea of blessings out of perceived cursings make you feel?

1.3

THE DIFFICULTY OF JESUS

*It was only yesterday that you outsiders to God's ways had
no idea of any of this, didn't know the first thing about the
way God works, hadn't the faintest idea of Christ.*

EPHESIANS 2:11-12

Know what's super annoying? When you know *exactly* what
a friend needs to do, *should* do, and that friend . . . does
something else. Come on! Can't you just listen to someone
who knows what's best for you?

It's like when I was an assistant pastor in beautiful Marin
County, California, at the tender age of twenty-four. I was
also single. Now I may not be the best-looking dude around,
but I discovered that didn't stop some awkward stuff from
going down. Like I'd be talking to someone after the service,
encouraging them about something, and they'd say, "That
reminds me, pastor, have you met my daughter? The one
who's holy and beautiful?"

And the dinner invitations! At that stage in life, I always
agreed to a free meal, home-cooked or not. But half the time
I'd arrive to find four places: two for the host couple, one for
me, and one for their daughter. What do you do with *that*? I
know what *I* did. I ate like I hadn't had a good meal in ages
(which was true), skipped seconds (much to my own cha-
grin), and hastily exited under some false pretense of spiritual
service. I know, I know, I'm a sinner, but that's why I believe

in Jesus! (Not to mention the follow-up conversation the next Sunday! "So what did you think of my daughter?" "She was . . . ah . . . she was . . . she was *nice*. Yeah, so . . . um . . . how can I pray for you?")

Anyway, my pastor and his family were an integral part of my life back then. God used Pastor John Henry Corcoran in some profound ways, both as a friend and mentor—plus, he had one wicked sense of humor! His wife, Hilary, was like a big sister to me, and like any big sister she was quite concerned with my relationship status. She had her eyes on a young gal in the congregation named Lynn, and Hilary was sure that Lynn was perfect for me. She wasn't quiet about her opinion, either. She skated pretty close to actually *harassing* me about it. "Daniel, Lynn is *perfect* for you. She loves God, she's beautiful, she's kind—I mean, she's the opposite of you!" (Don't you love backhanded compliments?)

Hilary *knew* that Lynn and I would be great together, but all she got was the Fusco stonewall. I continually told her to leave me alone about that. I wasn't interested. Not one bit.

Until I married Lynn, of course. Hilary knew it long before I ever did, but I couldn't, or wouldn't, see it at the time.

Jesus actually frustrated his disciples and friends in a way similar to how I frustrated Hilary. They knew what he should be doing, but he stubbornly refused to see their wisdom. (Don't take the analogy too far, though—Jesus was actually right, whereas I was stubborn and oh-so-wrong.)

Ever heard of the guy called Lazarus in the Bible? He's

famous for two reasons: His sisters were Mary and Martha, who get spoken about an awful lot in the life of Jesus, plus he was almost the start of an actual zombie apocalypse.

Jesus was great friends with Mary and Martha and Lazarus. And one day, as we read in John 11, Lazarus got sick—not the kind where you have soup and watch reruns on the couch, but the kind of sick where you're going to end up dead. So the sisters send a message to Jesus, implying that he should hurry over to their village and sort things out.

Naturally, Jesus stays put for two more days. And *then* he says to his disciples, "Let's go see Lazarus."

At which point the disciples are like, "Wait, Lazarus from the town of Bethany? Because last time we were there, some of the locals tried to stone you, right? So . . ."

Jesus sort of shakes his head, and tells them that he's walking in God's light, not to mention Lazarus is only sleeping, and if they head over to Bethany, they can wake him up.

Thomas, who'd later be famous for his doubts, is fired up. He would have tweeted, "Let's *do* this! We're all going to die if we go there, but you only live once!"

And so off they go.

Trouble is, by the time they arrive, all dusty toes and parched throats, Lazarus has already been dead for half a week, and the mourning is in full-wail. Martha meets Jesus at the outskirts of the town, away from the mourners, and says, "If you'd been here sooner, our brother wouldn't have died. But even now, God will give you whatever you pray for."

"Lazarus is going to rise," he tells her.

"I know, I know—at the end of time," Martha says. "We're *all* going to rise again in the resurrection." Jesus' words seem like cold comfort to Martha, the kind of thing someone says to you at a funeral that doesn't actually help you feel any better.

Jesus comes back at her with, "I *am* the resurrection and the life. Anyone who believes in me will live, even if they die—and if you live by believing in me, you'll never die. Do you believe that?"

Martha gives the right answer: "Yes, Lord. I believe you're the Messiah, God's Son."

Other than Jesus, no one's quite sure what the plan is at this point. Lazarus is dead, Martha is grieving, and the disciples are on the lookout for the stoners—the rock-wielding mob—and now it's Mary's turn to talk with Jesus.

She falls at his feet and lets it all hang out, weeping and pointing out the obvious fact that if Jesus had showed up sooner, her brother—and Jesus' friend—would still be alive. Now *all* the other mourners are arriving, having followed Mary out of the house, and Jesus is surrounded. He also begins to weep, and shaken to his core, he asks to see Lazarus's grave.

On the way, everyone notices how grief-stricken Jesus is, leading some to marvel at how much he must have loved the deceased. Others, though, know Jesus' reputation for working miracles, and they say things like, "He opened the eyes of a blind man a few weeks back—you're telling me he couldn't have healed Lazarus if he'd been here sooner?"

Now let's hit pause on the story here for a minute.

If you've heard Bible stories before, you might be forgiven for thinking that they're all kind of boring. We preachers are partially to blame. We've tended to focus on the *point* of the story, on the moral lesson, and in the process we've shortchanged the actual *stories*. Which, sometimes, are just weird!

So check out what's happening in this one. Don't give it a pass just because it's about Jesus. Like, "Oh well, everything Jesus does is perfect and makes perfect sense. Because, you know, *Jesus*."

But does this story make any sense so far?

Think of how Jesus' friends could have helped him make everything simpler. They knew what would make sense, even if he apparently didn't. Mary and Martha sent word that Lazarus was sick, because they knew if Jesus got there fast enough, Lazarus would recover. The disciples knew that going into an area where there were people waiting to kill them was a bad idea. And the list goes on and on.

It makes you wonder. Is Jesus being purposefully difficult in this story? And if so, does God do that same kind of thing to us today? When there seems to be a clear-cut solution to the messiness of life, and we've got everything figured out, why does God seem to do something so . . . different? Or sometimes nothing at all?

These are live questions. They are also volatile. Many people have fled faith in God because questions like these can be a sucker punch to the face of casual faith. I don't ask them to immediately answer them. I'm asking them so we can see what's at stake when the messiness of life collides with the God who reigns over the mess.

Let's see how the story concludes. Jesus is still a wreck. That might sound like something you can't say about Jesus, but think about what the text is telling us. Bible translators use phrases to describe Jesus like "once more deeply moved" (John 11:38, NIV) and "troubled in spirit" (verse 33, ISV). What do those mean? Jesus was God, but he was also 100 percent human—that's one of the messy ways we understand God, which we'll look at more on page 58. So as a human being, Jesus was being confronted by a lot of what we might call *stressors*. Two of his good friends, Mary and Martha, were mourning for their dead brother and basically accusing Jesus of not getting there fast enough to rescue him. Jesus had lost Lazarus too—not as a brother, but as a friend—not to mention Jesus knew there were a bunch of people who wanted to kill him!

So that's how Jesus ends up standing outside of Lazarus's sealed tomb, weeping.

His friends—and we—know what Jesus should do. Finish mourning, comfort Mary and Martha, and move on. It's obvious, right? Life's messy. People die too early. It sucks. But what are you going to do?

Well, that question always has *way* more possible answers when we ask it of Jesus!

"Take away the stone," he says.

Martha is shocked. And probably offended. Her brother

is dead, no thanks to Jesus, and now he's asking for the tomb to be *opened*? "But he's been in there *four* days," she says significantly, willing Jesus to understand what he's asking. She spells it out, though, just so everything is crystal clear. "It's . . . going to *stink*."

As he often does, Jesus comes back at her with a question: "Didn't I tell you that if you believe, you'll see God's glory?"

How's Martha going to answer that? She nods, and a half dozen guys step out of the crowd and move the stone away, unsealing the tomb. Now what? The tension is thick as fog.

"Father," Jesus says, his face tipped toward the sky, "thank you for hearing me. I know you *always* hear me, but not everyone here today believes that. Maybe now they will."

Then, in a loud voice, he calls into the tomb. "Lazarus, come out!"

What follows is one of the longest shortest moments in the history of the world. And then one person in the crowd gasps—a teenager with 20/15 vision maybe—and pretty soon everyone is gasping. Because there's a mummy walking out of the tomb![2]

Then Jesus says one more thing: "Unwrap him so he can go."

And then . . . well, we don't know! The Bible contains a *lot* of messy stories, but the ending of this one is perhaps too messy, even for John, the Gospel writer who recorded it for us. We can guess, but we wouldn't have a lot to go on.

---

[2] Good thing Jesus only called out Lazarus, or he really *would* have been the start of a zombie invasion.

Lazarus is alive, for sure, and everyone knows it. Jesus has once again proved that nothing—*nothing*—is out of reach for him when it comes to power, yet at the same time, he has shown a vulnerable, emotional side that might not match what people think about him.

We see the division immediately, because in the verse following, John tells us that many of the people who had come to comfort Mary and Martha chose to believe that Jesus was their promised Messiah, the one who had come to fulfill all the hopes and dreams of humanity. You can probably guess why John uses the words *many people* though, right?

Because it wasn't everyone. The rest run off to the religious authorities to tattle. And the religious authorities plot to kill Jesus.

That's the way it worked with Jesus: save a friend, make a hundred enemies. Talk about messy. As they say, "No good deed ever goes unpunished."

Then again, Jesus has different ideas than we do about how to live life in the mess.

That is one of the reasons life can be so frustrating. Because God is unpredictable and works in strange ways. Like we saw with Jesus and the resurrection of Lazarus—would *any* of us have chosen *that* to be the way things should go? Nope!

But God is unique and works uniquely. God's ideas don't necessarily match *our* ideas for a great plan, and God rarely engages the *mess* in a way that we would consider *neat*.

RIFFING ON DIFFICULTY

- Where in your life is Jesus being difficult right now?
- Why do you think Jesus is working that way, as opposed to neatly and easily?

1.4

ROCKIN' A LIMP

When it came to presenting the Message to people who had no background in God's way, I was the least qualified of any of the available Christians. God saw to it that I was equipped, but you can be sure that it had nothing to do with my natural abilities.

EPHESIANS 3:8

Our ideas about healing are often limited to the absence of anything negative, whereas Jesus sees something negative as soil from which *real* healing can grow.

It reminds me of Jacob, in the Old Testament. He was the grandson of Abraham and the son of Isaac. Jacob, who would become one of the famed patriarchs of the nation of Israel, happened to be a swindler, a cheater, and a mama's boy, a kid who wanted to profit from everyone else's hard work. One night, before he's scheduled to meet his estranged older brother for the first time since cheating him out of his blessing, Jacob is visited by an angel of God—and that angel wrestles with Jacob and pops him one in the hip!

So Jacob gets up the next day with a limp, and the limp never goes away. Most of us would say that intervention from God made Jacob *worse*, not better. Except catch this: God also changed Jacob's name that night to *Israel* (Genesis 32:28), a name that means "governed by God."[3] Names are powerful, and something negative—like an angelically tweaked hip— can be the source of a changed life. Jacob went on to follow God's lead into great things, limping all the way.

I guess God likes his kids with a limp sometimes.

When God gives one of us a limp, we often become self-conscious about our uniqueness. We make excuses for our limp. But eventually, our God-given limp can become a type of swagger. Testing produces testimony. You know when you see someone with swagger that they've got a strength inside. God doesn't give his kids a limp out of boredom, but so that they can develop confidence in him.

Like before I started following Jesus, you know what I hated? The church. Those hypocritical religious types. Which is why I cursed out a priest in my driveway this one time.

It was the summer of 1997, hot and humid like always on our middle-class cul-de-sac in central New Jersey.

But I was hotter. Mom was on hospice care with her cancer, and her priest was visiting her, and he was *not* on my good side.

See, Mom *loved* the beach. We grew up going "down the shore" to Long Beach Island. In between baseball games and summer theater workshops, all summer long. We had a little

---

[3] David Guzik, "Commentary on Isaiah 48," *David Guzik Commentaries on the Bible*, http://www .studylight.org/commentaries/guz/view.cgi?bk=22&ch=48 (accessed July 14, 2015).

place down there we loved, and as usual, we were always surrounded by family and friends. And mom would always wear her favorite T-shirt.

Life's a beach . . . and then you die.

So naturally she wanted to be cremated and have her ashes sprinkled on the beach at LBI. We wanted that too.

And that was the plan, at least until the priest came by that day.

Mom was fragile in every way imaginable. She was struggling with her own mortality, she wasn't sleeping well, she was losing weight. So when Mom explains the cremation plan, and the beach she loves and may never see again, the priest informs her that it wouldn't be a *proper* Christian burial. And proceeds to try to sell my parents space in a sacred church mausoleum, with special family deals if they bought a whole block.

I caught up to the priest as he was about to climb into his car.

"Hey, can I talk to you for a minute? Why can't my mother have her ashes scattered at the beach?"

"It's not a proper Christian burial."

"Well, I don't know that Bible of yours at all, but doesn't it say something like we come from dust and we go to dust? That sure sounds like what she wants to do, and she just *loves* the beach. Loves it!"

"Well, son, according to our church tradition, that is not a proper Christian burial."

My simmering, nineteen-year-old, scared-to-lose-my-mom heart exploded.

To my shame, I called him a lot of words I don't want to repeat now. I accused him of trying to profit from my mother's death. I informed him, in no uncertain terms, that he should be ashamed of himself. I mean, *how could he do that to us?* To her!

I was never, *never* going to get involved with church or religion or God, if this was what the whole thing was about. Not in a thousand lifetimes.

So after I started following Jesus, and as I was learning how to live in the mess, do you know what Jesus did? He gave me a limp. He used that negative view of the church I had, and he invited me to walk *into* that mess even further. To become a *pastor*! Because that was the negative soil from which real healing would grow. Not only for myself, but for others in the church.

Life is messy, and sometimes it feels like Jesus is the one doing the messing.

Maybe that's because he is.

RIFFING ON THE LIMP

- What limp has Jesus given you?
- Can you think of any ways God might be using that limp in your life? In other people's lives?

1.5

BECOMING UNBROKEN

He thought of everything, provided for everything we could possibly
need, letting us in on the plans he took such delight in making.
He set it all out before us in Christ, a long-range plan in which
everything would be brought together and summed up in him,
everything in deepest heaven, everything on planet earth.

EPHESIANS 1:8-10

For many of us, *many* of us, the issue with God is that somewhere along life's way, we prayed that he would do something—and he didn't. So we've concluded that God isn't worth trusting, or asking. Or simply that God doesn't exist. Better off to trust ourselves. Even if we fail time after time, at least we're predictable. At least we won't get our hopes up, only to have them crushed.

I wonder what Mary and Martha thought when Jesus showed up late, after their brother had already died. I wonder what Mary and Martha thought after Jesus brought their brother back to life . . . and they became the family with the guy who used to be dead. It wasn't simple. It wasn't understandable. *Their* plan made a lot more sense than what Jesus actually chose to do.

Here's the truth: God's purposes and plans sometimes—often?—don't run in the same direction as ours.

We feel like it's wrong to admit, "God, I *struggle* with the fact that you _____."

It isn't wrong, but since we think it is, we can become bitter.

We continue to think God did wrong by us, because we continue to think that God should have followed *our* way instead.

I'm not going to contradict that, per se. But I am going to ask a question we often leave unasked. If we claim our ways would have been better for God to follow, we're making an assumption: that we are both wiser and more loving than God. So here's the question:

Have you ever lived an entire day with perfect love and perfect wisdom?

I've never even lived an hour like that! Honestly, I've never even lived a *minute* like that!

So I'm learning to give God the benefit of the doubt on the whole purposes-and-plans thing. I'm learning to be able to trust God—a God who is more mysterious than many of my religious colleagues are willing to let on. I'm learning that it really isn't even necessary for me to have "clarity" on the mess. I'm willing to admit, at least when I'm being honest, that I might not fully understand the extent of God's love and wisdom. That maybe God can see the mess better than I can. And not just see it, but deal with it. Transform and redeem it.

But *dang*. Sometimes trusting him to do that feels impossibly hard, doesn't it?

RIFFING ON TRUST

- Complete this sentence: "God, I *struggle* with the fact that you _____."
- Is it hard for you to trust that God can transform and redeem your mess? Why or why not?

1.6

CAN I GET A REMEDY?

*I greet you with the grace and peace poured into our lives
by God our Father and our Master, Jesus Christ.*

EPHESIANS 1:2

Some of you are already frustrated. I know you are. You're all about action. You're like, "I know, I know, my life is messy, but what should I *do?*" You want the correct tool so you can make the necessary changes. You're the people who make lists just so you can check stuff off 'em. So I'll tell you. Let's solve this.

Read this verse, from the apostle Paul's letter to the Ephesians:

"Grace to you and peace from God our Father and the Lord Jesus Christ" (ESV).

Boom. You're welcome.

The remedy for the mess is grace and peace.

Now that we've solved that for all you activity junkies, feel free to skip ahead to whatever chapter seems the most interesting. Ephesians has a lot of rad stuff in it, and we pretty much tour through all of it![4]

So yeah, grace and peace. That's God's prescription for how the messiness of life can be transformed, through Jesus. Grace and peace. Grace and peace. The remedy for the mess is grace and peace.

---

[4] I'm a big fan of the stuff about walking bass lines that starts on page 79, if you're looking for a recommendation.

Now, while those action heroes rush off to start gracing-and-peacing everything, the rest of us can read on—and we need it!

Let's look at those two words, *grace* and *peace*. Grace and peace. (Wondering why I repeat them so often? Because God does, and I'm just following that lead! The New Testament uses those two words together fourteen times.)

So *grace*. Grace isn't an exclusively Christian concept. At the time Paul was writing his letter to the followers of Jesus who lived in the city of Ephesus, the idea of grace was well established. All the way back to guys like Aristotle and Plato, you see the term *grace* used to describe something that is given, absolutely freely, with no expectation of return. Everyone understood grace to be about a generous gift, something you received for no reason, and something you couldn't pay back—even if you wanted to. So that was the sketch on which Paul elaborated the Christian concept of grace.

Peace is a complicated word too, even though it seems simple. Peace is far more than the absence of conflict. The best way to understand biblical peace is with the Hebrew word *shalom*, which means both "peace" and "to join." The implication is that when something is separated, or broken, it needs to be fixed.

A relationship is separated, but then joined back together.

A bone is broken, but then joined back together.

"Shalom" also happened to be the standard Hebrew greeting and salutation.

I remember a kid from our church who went on vacation

to Texas, and he came back with a shirt that said, "Shalom, y'all!" Wouldn't it be great if we rocked more shirts like that? Shalom is all about putting things back together, and even better than before. If two people are fighting, biblical peace doesn't mean they simply stop fighting; it means they are united in relationship.

With grace and peace, then, we've got a generous, undeserved gift, linked up with the redemptive and restorative joining together of what is separated or broken. Becoming *un*broken.

Know anyone who could use that combo? Could you? Just talking about this gives me hope.

And notice that in the New Testament, it's always grace and peace, not peace and grace. I don't think that's an accident. I don't have anything against that famous English theologian, John Lennon, God rest his soul, but the problem with "give peace a chance" is that peace has *no* chance, *unless* it's preceded by grace. Only when grace is given and received first does peace becomes possible.

It's like Paul talks about in Ephesians 2:8-9, when he says, "For it is by grace you have been saved, through faith—and this is not from yourselves, it is the gift of God—not by works, so that no one can boast" (NIV). See, the saving is all in God's court. *All* of it. Grace isn't just the gift we receive for no reason; it's the gift that keeps on giving. When, by faith, we accept his gift, we are saved . . . and absolutely none of the credit goes to us!

The result, then, is that we close our mouths. No bragging,

because we didn't do diddly-squat! And rather than bragging, we get down to *living* in the glow of that grace—in the peace that is now possible.

Think of that cheesy bumper sticker that happens to be one-thousand-percent true: *No Jesus, No Peace. Know Jesus, Know Peace.* First comes God's grace—always God's grace—and only then does peace have a chance to follow. To flow out into our lives and the lives of those around us.

It isn't easy or simple. But by the literal grace of God, it becomes possible.

How many times have you tried to repair something that's been broken, without first having received the gift of grace? That peace is always short lived.

It's like when you have an issue in a friendship. It may not be anything enormous, but it's still a real issue, so you try to sweep it under the rug. *Try* to. Because the problem with sweeping things under the rug is that we don't expect the rug to have a pile under it, and eventually we trip over it, or the rug rips. At some point the rug has to be lifted, and the issue addressed for real. We've all tried to keep the peace without giving the gift of grace, and it doesn't work.

See, when *God's* grace grabs your heart, then you can go to somebody who's wronged you and you can truly offer peace. Because God has already given peace to you.

So the remedy for this mess is grace and peace. It comes from God, it's made possible by Jesus, and it's empowered by the Spirit—and it is something that we are meant to share with others.

If your life is messy, God wants to give you a gift: the transformational power to change "just a mess" into a glorious mess.

RIFFING ON THE REMEDY

- Describe grace and peace in your own words.
- Where in your life do you need some shalom?

1.7

REFLECTIONS ON A MESSY GOD

How blessed is God! And what a blessing he is! He's the Father of our Master, Jesus Christ, and takes us to the high places of blessing in him.

EPHESIANS 1:3

There's a key reason it's so hard for us to trust that God's *remedy for the mess* is God's grace and peace *in the mess.*

The reason is that our understanding of God's character, and what his character *means* for everything we're going through, is also messy.

As a pastor, I often get asked questions that are impossible to answer.

"How can this be God's plan?"

"Pastor, you need to ask God to fix this."

"How could a good God allow . . . ?"

"Where was God when . . . ?"

These are honest questions. I've asked them myself. Here's the thing about life, though. When stuff happens that we don't understand, we need to rely on what we *do* understand. So I often respond to these honest questions by reminding people that no one understands all of what God is doing. But at the same time, we do know for sure some other things that God is up to.

We know that God is good. God is love. God is sovereign. God is all powerful. God is full of compassion. Those are things we know.

In the midst of our messy lives, though? These truths about God are often challenged, or just plain-old tough to believe. There are no easy answers here.

In one of his letters to the followers of Jesus who lived in Corinth, Paul writes that "now we see in a mirror dimly" (1 Corinthians 13:12, ESV). The awesome mirror technology we experience every day when we're getting ready for work? That hadn't reached the common people two thousand years ago. If you wanted to look at yourself, and there wasn't a pool of water handy, you had to sort of squint into a flat hunk of polished metal.[5]

Point is, seeing in a "mirror dimly" in Bible times meant a strong emphasis on *dimly*. Paul was like, *The stuff you understand now? Trust me, that's like the teeniest taste of the whole pie!*

So let's connect that with the messiness of life. It's not that we can't know *anything* about life—why things happen, what's going to happen next, and that sort of thing—it's just that we can't know *everything*. We see only in a mirror dimly.

---

[5] Nowadays we even have those mirrors with built-in spotlights and magnifying technology, and every pore just pops out at you. My wife has one of those in our bathroom. Every so often I sneak a peek, and it's like the horror movie music starts playing—*Eee! Eee! Eee!*—and I run out screaming.

It's blurred. It's messy. It's not as neat as we'd like it to be. And you know what? Unfortunately, it's not going to get any better on this side of eternity.

That creates an even bigger mess for us in a culture like ours. A perusal of the side of any box of cereal allows us to know almost everything about what we're eating. Heck, along with the health information, we can even get a free recipe! But . . . how will the cereal make us feel later in the day? Is it genetically modified? What are the conditions like in the factory where it was made? Or on the farm where the ingredients were grown? What could we be eating instead?

We live in an information age, and all the information in the world is immediately at our fingertips. Yet how many of those details truly help us understand our own lives or how we should live? Honestly, a great deal of the information we are surrounded with *seems* important but is ultimately insignificant.

And all the while, the information we *really* want—like who God is and what God's ultimate purposes are in the midst of the mess—remains elusive.

Take the biblical doctrine of the Trinity: God existing in three distinct persons—Father, Son, and Spirit—but still as one God. There isn't a book of the Bible where that idea is laid out, step by step, like a textbook or systematic theology.[6] Now, over the last two thousand years, some extremely wise and careful and prayerful and creative folks have generally agreed that the God of the Bible is triune, three parts, but still one

---

[6] Although Ephesians 1:3-14 is an extraordinarily succinct look at it, written by the apostle Paul with an awesome run-on sentence that will make the English teachers out there face-palm!

person. However, despite my belief in that—and I *do* think it's the best way to explain who God is and how God has been revealed to us in Scripture and nature—it's not as neat as I'd like it to be. I wish it was easier to understand, and easier to explain when folks sit in my office and ask me about it!

But just because our understanding of the Trinity is messy doesn't mean we can't know *anything* about God's nature. Again, "not everything" is a far cry from "not anything."

Let's start with something we *can* know. The Bible is the story of God, just like it's the story of us. And God tells us a lot about who we are in the midst of the mess.

RIFFING ON NOT KNOWING

- What about God is hard for you to understand?
- What about God do you understand?

1.8

BAD NEWS FIRST

It was only yesterday that you outsiders to God's ways had no idea of any of this, didn't know the first thing about the way God works, hadn't the faintest idea of Christ.

EPHESIANS 2:11

"What do you want to hear first: the good news or the bad news?"

I can't stand it when people ask me that. I always want to hear the bad news first, because if I *know* I'm going to get bad news, I want to get it out of the way, right? And I also hope that once it's out of the way, the good news will do a little something to counteract it. Like when my doctor asks me that, and then gives that stern-doctor look and says, like House, "Fusco, your cholesterol is high enough to make bacon worry"—then right away I can say, "Sure, sure, so you're saying I shouldn't put Bac-Os on my breakfast cereal, got it . . . so anyway, what's the good news?"

That is my preferred order for news, but you know why I can't stand it? Because no matter how good the good news is, it's kind of poisoned by the bad news. Like you can put a few drops of lemon juice in my coffee, or you can put half a cup of lemon juice in my coffee, but either way, it's not going to taste nearly as good as a strong Americano from Lava Java, where my friend Phuong pulls the best shots.

But I get the instinct. There's actually some grace to that, some goodwill. Because the instinct isn't to ruin the good news—it's to soften the bad news.

So I'm giving you the biblical bad news first.

You know how *biblical* has become a synonym for *epic* or *profound*? As in, "I'm gonna put a beat down on you of *biblical* proportions!"[7] In this case, that's a very good definition of biblical. Because the bad news—the biblical bad news— is seriously, profoundly bad. It's just the worst ever.

But the good news? That's also of *seriously* biblical proportions. It's so good that it'll make up for the bad news, I promise. But the catch is that we can't skip right to the good

---

[7] That was just an example . . . I'm a lover, not a fighter.

news, because it won't make any sense without the bad. So let me give it to you straight.

Here's the bad news: We are far, *far* worse than we realize.

Some of you are right with me. You're like, "Yeah, Fusco, got it. We're bad news. You're preaching to the choir. I've got a pretty low self-opinion already, thank you very much."

Others aren't buying it. You're like, "Speak for yourself, you hippie weirdo bass-playing pastor. I'm actually pretty good, all things considered. You want 'worse than you realize'? Try my cousin Charles—that guy is a piece of work!"

But our reaction can't change the fact that *all* of us are worse than we know.

Life is messy? Sure, we're on board. Amen, Brother Fusco!

But . . . *we* are messy? That can be much harder to swallow . . . even though we know, deep down, it's true.

I look at the messiness of life—all the circumstances and events and surprises—and it doesn't take the Behavioral Analysis Unit from the show *Criminal Minds* to conclude that the messiness usually stems from the *people* involved in the circumstances.[8]

I know that it isn't *always* true that people are the problem. Like if a tornado touches down, that wasn't because someone in the town screwed up. Or if my car breaks down, it isn't necessarily anyone's fault (unless, of course, it's due to my mechanical negligence). But a ton of the messy stuff in

---

[8] I'm pretty sure I've seen every episode of that show, and most episodes a bunch of times. But when I'm standing in front of God, I probably won't be bragging, "Yeah, Lord, I got to where I was like, almost an agent in the BAU because of my understanding of that TV show. I mean, I could profile anyone you need before you let them into heaven, so . . ." I'm just putting my stuff out there for you. Even my TV habits are messy!

life comes down to people. Job issues, breakups, fights with our kids or our parents, guilt trips . . . the list goes on and on.

And honestly? Sometimes the person who's increasing the mess for others . . . is me.

Okay, not sometimes. Often. Heck, *most* of the time!

The Bible actually tells us that we are *dead* in our messiness. Not just contributing to the mess while we keep on sailing, but dead in the water.[9] Dead in what some versions of the Bible call our "trespasses" and "sins," which is how God views our overt acts of messiness and even our naive mistakes.

We're often told that we should be more positive. And positivity can be a good thing! But sometimes we need an injection of realism. Not necessarily pessimism, but something close to it. Imagine waking up, stumbling into the bathroom, taking a bleary-eyed look in the mirror, and saying your morning mantra, all froggy-voiced, "You're a rebel and a total failure."

That's not usually the way I start my day! But that's exactly what I am. I rebel against God by nature, and I fail at living up to the standard God has created me for. So yeah, I *am* a rebel and a failure. I'm worse than I realize.

RIFFING ON THE BAD NEWS
- What are some ways you've increased someone else's mess?
- How do you feel, hearing that you're worse than you realize?

---

[9]More on how we solve that dead issue in several chapters, so keep reading. Unless you don't really care about coming back to life.

CULTURAL CANCER

The Messiah has made things up between us so that we're now together on this, both non-Jewish outsiders and Jewish insiders. He tore down the wall we used to keep each other at a distance. He repealed the law code that had become so clogged with fine print and footnotes that it hindered more than it helped. Then he started over. Instead of continuing with two groups of people separated by centuries of animosity and suspicion, he created a new kind of human being, a fresh start for everybody.

EPHESIANS 2:14-15

You know what would be great? Finally getting to the good news.

Instead? Here's another round of bad news for you. You're welcome. But before you get frustrated with me, remember we're being honest here. And it isn't honest to give you only the sunny side of the story. A light always shines brightest in the darkness.

We haven't gone quite deep enough into the bad news yet. I want to dig into the notion that we are rebels and failures, and I want to tunnel in two distinct but related directions. First we'll look at how we, as individuals, are rebels and failures, and then we'll look at how that inevitably transfers to society.

It's so interesting that knowing Jesus is often the *only* way we can see that we were living the wrong way.

When we try to evaluate ourselves, and fix ourselves, without Jesus, it's as effective as the person who proudly announces,

"I made a complete 360-degree turn in my life!" So . . . you went from facing the wrong direction . . . back to facing in the exact same wrong direction!

But that's what happens when we're on our own. Without Jesus, who is the Way, we can't see where we need to be going, and we can't see where we are, which means that we end up wandering in circles, back to where we started every time.

And if we try to pretend we're not messy? Then we've got a whole identity problem going on, and I can't think of *anything* messier than trying to pretend that you aren't messy! Talk about a total train wreck of a mess!

If we commit ourselves to the fallacy that *we* aren't the problem, then we must also commit to seeing *others* as the bad ones. We judge, look down our noses, all because we're trying to hold up a facade of togetherness.

That was me before I met Jesus. I thought of myself as a pretty good guy up through college. Sure, I did drugs, and slept around, and lied and cheated—an all-around great guy!—but who *didn't* do that as a teenager and young adult? I loved my family, and I tried to learn in school, and I was a decent friend. So if I thought about the future direction of my life, it was in terms of tweaks. Minor course corrections. Basically my life would be more of the same, except I'd do it a bit better or smarter.

When I met Jesus, the scales fell from my eyes.[10] Suddenly it was like, "I *can't* believe I used to *do* that!" Or think, value,

---

[10] If you think about it, that's a creepy expression, from Acts 9:18. There is some seriously weird stuff in the Bible, which I love!

promote, and chase that. I suddenly saw that my entire life was
. . . gone. Way gone. Far out, jacked up, straight-up wrong!

That's a story I've heard over and over, both from people
you'd label as "sinners" *and* people you'd label as "saints."
Actually, you probably wouldn't even use those words. You
would say "good" people and "bad" people. And that's the
key point here: *Anyone* who follows Jesus will see their life in
a new way, *no matter how they used to live.*

There's a great line from a song by Steve Taylor that goes,
"Jesus is for losers."[11] So true! Jesus told the religious leaders
of his day, "Hey, it isn't healthy people who need a doctor, but sick people!" (Luke 5:31, author's paraphrase). Same
idea. What we learn when we follow Jesus—when the Spirit
shows us the truth of our lives—is that we're *all* sick. We're
all losers. That's the *aha* moment at the heart of what Jesus
is saying.

Jesus is for losers, and all of us are losers.

So Jesus is for *us*.

Which really maps out the whole "rebels and failures"
thing across all of humanity! And that's the second idea we're
digging into: that the bad news extends as far and wide as
the human race. There aren't good people and bad people
in life; there are only messy people, and messy people make
messy families and neighborhoods and towns and cultures
and countries.

Do you know anyone who looks back on the "glory days"?[12]

---

[11]Steve Taylor, "Jesus Is for Losers," *Squint* © 1993 Warner Alliance.
[12]I can hear the Boss's opening guitar lick to "Glory Days" playing in the background, can't you?
  Dun dun nah nah. Dun dun nah nah.

People talk about how much better it used to be, back then, when everyone was so much more hardworking and decent and honest. That sounds great, doesn't it? Wouldn't it be wonderful to return to a time like that?

Only problem is that it's not true. There has *never* been a time like that. See, Jesus has never reigned fully in any one *culture*, ever—yet Jesus reigns in the *people* of God who have been called out of every culture.

There's never been a generation that followed Jesus, because a generation *can't* follow Jesus. *People* can follow Jesus.[13]

I've had this exact conversation multiple times.

Older person: "I just don't understand young people today!"

Me: "Man, you're right!"

Older person: *shaking head regretfully*

Me: "Know what though? Your parents said the same thing about your generation, and their parents said the same thing about their generation."

Older person: *staring at me like I'm insane*

Me: "And guess what? When today's kids become parents, they're going to be like, 'I don't understand young people today!'"

Realistically, there's never been an age or a culture that wasn't in rebellion against God. Nazi Germany? Rebellion

---

13 Which reminds me, what's the deal with using *Christian* as an adjective for non-people? We hear about Christian restaurants and countries and colleges. There may be a high number of Christian people at or in those organizations, but the organizations themselves can't follow Jesus.

against God. Communist Russia? Rebellion against God. But those are easy ones.

Now what about twenty-first-century America? Rebellion against God. And most of you are probably still with me: *Yeah, our country has strayed from its godly heritage. It's like 2 Chronicles 7:14 says: "If my people who are called by my name humble themselves, and pray and seek my face and turn from their wicked ways, then I will hear from heaven and will forgive their sin and heal their land"* (ESV). So if we return to how we *used* to be, in previous generations, God will bless our nation, right?

Not so fast. Without going too far down the rabbit hole, this verse was written to Israel about 2,500 years ago. America is not ancient Israel, and crucially, *we who follow Jesus are not living under the national, Old Testament law of Moses.* The New Testament makes it clear that the gospel can't be confined by national boundaries. Every *person* has equal access to God, through Jesus, and on the flip side, no *nation* has access to God. Nations—like Christian restaurants, but *un*like all dogs—don't go to heaven.

So twenty-first-century America? Rebellion against God. Just like twentieth-century America, nineteenth-century America, eighteenth-century America, and every other nation and culture and society in history, ever.

What that means is that if we follow Jesus, and we see the failure and rebellion in our own lives for the first time, we can also see the failure and rebellion in the society we're part of.

All of us are born into a culture, a society, and every

culture has unique values. It's usually easy for us to pick out the negative values in a foreign culture—like, "China's brutal repression of free speech is wrong!"—but more difficult to pick out the positive values, such as China's respect for the elderly. And in our own culture, the opposite tends to be true: We cherry-pick positive values, but we're shocked—*shocked!*—if someone points out a negative value.[14]

Okay, we've been digging, but it's time for two paragraphs' worth of *serious* spelunking. There's some deep stuff on tap for us right now. But trust me, it'll be worth our while to explore. First there's this, about the danger of thinking that when it comes to culture, our way is the only way. One of the greatest minds of the twentieth century, a British professor named Clive Staples Lewis—who naturally went by "C. S."—warned against "the uncritical acceptance of the intellectual climate common to our own age,"[15] something we looked at in the last paragraph. But his words also give us a reason *why* that happens: We assume that "whatever has gone out of date is on that account discredited."[16] Like, if it's old, I don't want to know it, man! Lewis called that "chronological snobbery"[17] and recognized that *every* age has "characteristic illusions" and "widespread assumptions which are so ingrained in the age that no one dares to attack or feels it necessary to defend them."[18]

---

[14] *cough* *Unfettered capitalism is not rooted in the Greatest Commandment and the Golden Rule perpetuates idolatry, pride, and economic injustice.* *cough*

[15] C. S. Lewis, *Surprised by Joy* (San Diego: Harcourt, 1955), 207.

[16] Lewis, *Surprised by Joy,* 207.

[17] Lewis, *Surprised by Joy,* 207.

[18] Lewis, *Surprised by Joy,* 208.

Deep! And here in our second spelunking paragraph, let's give a definition to those illusions and assumptions, because no matter when and where we live, there is a way we all walk and talk, even without realizing it, right? One commentator describes the spirit of the age this way: "That floating mass of thoughts, opinions, maxims, speculations, hopes, impulses, aims, aspirations . . . which constitute a most real and effective power; being the moral, or immoral, atmosphere which at every moment of our lives we inhale, again inevitably to exhale."[19]

Now wasn't that a fun side trip? And now you can quote Lewis to your friends and get major nerd-props. It's true though: We are so absorbed by our culture, so unaware of our own illusions and assumptions, that we can't help but breathe in our cultural values. *Just as we can't help breathe them out!*

And here's where we come back to the surface. Just as Jesus allows us to see our own blindness, so Jesus is the only vantage point by which we can see *past* or *outside* our own culture. It's as if following Jesus gives us an oxygen mask, and when we put it on and breathe deeply, for the first time we aren't breathing in and out our pure host culture. We're breathing God's Spirit instead.

So the bad news is worse than we realize. It's *exceedingly* bad news, matter of fact. We're individual rebels and failures, we're corporate rebels and failures, and without Jesus we can't even *see* a way out, let alone actually escape.

---

[19] R. C. Trench, *Synonyms of the New Testament* (London: Kegan Paul, 1886), 218.

RIFFING ON CULTURE
- How is the way of Jesus different from the way of your culture?
- How are you breathing in the spirit of your culture?

1.10

CHOOSE HOPE

Christ brought us together through his death on the cross. The Cross got us to embrace, and that was the end of the hostility. Christ came and preached peace to you outsiders and peace to us insiders. He treated us as equals, and so made us equals. Through him we both share the same Spirit and have equal access to the Father.

EPHESIANS 2:16-18

You're sick of the bad news by now, right? You're sick of talking about the messiness. Maybe you're trying to understand what God is calling you to do with your life. Or you can't imagine staying married for one more minute. Or you have to go to the hospital every day because that's where your kid is living. And you're all, *Okay, stop telling me how bad things are and just tell me what I can do.*

Want to know what I'd say?

On second thought, maybe I shouldn't tell you. I know it'll make some of you angry. Others will chuckle with disbelief. Some mouths will tighten, and you'll still be polite, but you'll be thinking, *If I had a dollar for every time I heard* that *cliché.*

So you have permission to skip ahead. I won't blame you. If you're still reading, though, here it goes.

"This is hard, and I know it doesn't seem like it makes any sense. But what happens next is up to you: You can get bitter or you can get better."

Right after I lost my mother, I ended up alone, back at my college apartment. And I remember feeling like things had basically shut down and turned off. The taste and flavor of life had disappeared. Every color was a shade of gray. So I climbed into my bed with my clothes on, and I pulled the covers up over my head. *I'm not leaving*, I told myself. *This is where I'm gonna stay.*

Two hours later, I suddenly tossed back the covers and sat up. *What the heck am I doing—Mom would* kill *me if she saw me doing this!*

That was the prompt I needed. I got up from my bed and got on with life.

But here's the thing: Life didn't get easier. I was still crushed by losing my mom. Destroyed. Like a house where the foundation had just been swept away, and it was only a matter of time until I collapsed. My circumstances did not change one bit between the time I climbed in bed and climbed back out.

But here's the *other* thing: Even though life didn't get easier, *I didn't get bitter.* And what that meant was that I was giving myself the *chance*, by God's grace, to get better.

Circumstances can change in an instant. Better and bitter change over the course of a lifetime.

Maybe you're reading this and thinking, *Give it a rest.*

You're jaded. You've given God all the chances you care to, and you're pretty sure things aren't going to get better.

If that's you, then listen: There is *no* judgment here. No judgment.

Honestly. Feel free to be messy here with me. What I have for you isn't an agenda, but a collection of thoughts and stories that, I believe, lead toward hope. Not easy answers, but hope. I believe that that's why you picked up this book and why you've made it this far. I believe God planned that. I believe God loves you so much, there's no such thing as "too late." (Though I can't *prove* that of course. Remember how messy life is?)

Listen, if you were to give your life to Jesus *right now*— like, put down the book and walk out under the vast sky and just say, "Jesus, I need you. Help me. Save me. I want to know you and follow you"—guess what would change?

Nothing.

At least nothing in the *circumstances* of your life. The things that hurt you right now may still hurt. The things you don't understand may still be mysteries.

So what's the point?

The point is that nothing changes when you follow Jesus—and *everything* changes when you follow Jesus.

Your circumstances may not change, but *you* change. You change because you come into relationship with the God of your mess. The most substantial and holistic shift imaginable in your life will have just taken place—but not in the externals. Not the details, but in the *substance* of who you are.

Think of yourself as a tree: The point is that your DNA changes, like from a crab-apple tree to an apple tree. You may not bear fruit right away, but it becomes *possible* to bear fruit. Sweet fruit, if you can believe it. Fruit you can enjoy. Fruit that can be shared and given away. Fruit to be grateful for.

Each one of us stands at a crossroads, every single moment of our lives.

Bitter or better.

It's not a "choose once and forget about it" deal. Life might be going great for you right now, but something's going to force you to choose, tomorrow, next week, next year.

Bitter or better. Part of being created in God's image means having the ability—sometimes it feels more like a terrible privilege—to choose. God doesn't force us to do anything.

This is hard. For some it can be terribly, crushingly hard.

That's part of the messiness of life. You and I both know someone who has been absolutely bent over backward by bitterness. Maybe it's you.

But there's this picture given to us in the book of Isaiah of a dry reed, already bent and bruised, tipping toward the mud—and then God takes that fragile reed and restores it to life.

The good news of the Bible is that *no one* is beyond hope.

So choose to live with a messy understanding of God. Choose to believe there maybe is something like grace and peace in the mess. Choose hope. Because the good news is waiting.

RIFFING ON HOPE
- Where are you bitter right now?
- What areas of your life need hope infused into them?

CODA

How can we *not* feel beyond hope sometimes?

We're limping along, following God—yet God can seem difficult at times. We're aching for grace and peace, precisely because we're so aware of how much we need them. And always there's that temptation to get bitter. To just throw up our hands and surrender.

Except for that stubborn little corner of our hearts that's hardwired for hope. For what-ifs. What if there *is* a way to bring people together with people, and people together with God? What if *shalom* isn't just a funny Hebrew word, but a transformative way of life?

That's how God thinks too. Actually it's how God's *always* been thinking. It's like Ephesians 1:10-14 says: God didn't just make a long-range plan to unite *all* of creation in goodness and love . . . he absolutely *delighted* in making that plan, and then in making it happen!

God couldn't wait to bring his kids home.

Thing is, we mostly ask God to fix our messy circumstances, to fix all the junk that surrounds us and confounds us every day. But that rarely seems to happen.

I believe that's because God is more concerned with our hearts than our circumstances, and more concerned with what's inside us than outside us. We love the outcome, but God loves the process!

It's not that the outside doesn't matter. It does! But God's priority is our hearts. It's not entering the mess outside of us, but the *internal* mess, at the core of who we are.

It's a messy mix, to be sure, but it's the mix we're in.

So instead of using a magic wand to wave away all our external trouble, God's after something deeper. It's something we're all deeply familiar with: a journey. Journeys have ups and downs, highs and lows, but we take them for a reason: *to get somewhere we want to be.*

This messy life is both worse and better than we expect. Sometimes a lot worse, but in the end far better.

Jesus knew that deeply. He felt exactly the struggle that you feel. It's a ridiculous understatement to say that it wasn't easy to leave heaven's glory and become human. But he did it because he saw the end of the journey. "For the joy set before him," Hebrews 12:2 tells us, Jesus "endured the cross" (NIV).

He chose to go through the bad to get to the good—to go through the messy, unexplainable evil to get to the mind-bending, heart-exploding joy.

Ultimately that's what it's like for us, too.

As we'll begin to explore in the next section, Resolution, there's good news on the other side of the messiness, *and* good news *inside* the messiness. Life is a journey through that crazy mixture of messiness and joy.

And *into* pure joy. Because when we follow Jesus in the mess, that's where our journey will take us.

PART II
RESOLUTION

RESURRECTION

*God raised him from death and set him on a throne in deep heaven,
in charge of running the universe, everything from galaxies to governments,
no name and no power exempt from his rule. And not just for the time being,
but forever. He is in charge of it all, has the final word on everything.*

EPHESIANS 1:20-23

So that hope, that good news we've been waiting for? You can probably guess—it starts with Jesus.

When I was a kid, my parents gave me a wooden cross that had a plastic Jesus glued to it. Using a thumbtack, they stuck it above the door of my room. Having a cross on the wall was par for the course when you are all Italian. Once it was tacked up nice and straight, I glanced at it and then walked away without a second thought.

And I almost forgot all about it, except for one thing.

Jesus glowed in the dark, and that was *just* freaky enough to make me think. It would catch my eye when I went to the bathroom at night, or when I went to bed after watching TV with my parents. So when I moved out of my parents' house, I brought the crucifix with the plastic Jesus with me. Not because I wanted to worship it or anything, but just because I didn't really have anything else to do with it. I mean, I wasn't going to throw Jesus away, right?

Later, though, when I had become a Christian, I started to look at it more and more. And as I did, I realized something.

I didn't want that glowing plastic Jesus to be stuck on that cross anymore. So I popped him off with my thumbnail. I put the cross back up on my wall, and I put Jesus in a drawer.

Now I didn't know a thing back then, trust me! I wasn't really making a theological point—especially putting Jesus in a drawer!

But think about that image: Jesus *on* the cross, and then Jesus *off* the cross.

The cross gives way to a tomb, and here's the good news, the hope for us in this messy life: The tomb always gives way to an *empty* tomb.

We *can* live resurrection lives, following our resurrected Lord. God wants to do new things in us. Life is messy, but God is real. God is the God of the mess, Jesus is alive, and God's Spirit is loose in the world, transforming hearts and minds.

See, bitterness can grow because many of us just believe in a crucified Savior. Hope grows when we believe in a resurrected Lord.

If we follow a resurrected Lord, will our future be neat and tidy? Never. But when we walk on the path Jesus is showing us, God's Spirit empowers us to live resurrection lives. That's no small deal. It means that in the messiness, we're asking God what greater purpose might be at work. It means we're walking side-by-side with Jesus, who's lived through a messy life, just like us, and understands what we're going through.

God absolutely *loves* to do this: to draw us toward grace and peace in the midst of the mess.

I believe that there are some of you reading this right now, and God is saying to you, "I want to bring you back and I want to make you new! When my Son Jesus died on the cross, I was thinking of you, and I want to seal the deal by giving you the guarantee and the power of my Spirit. Right now!"

Life is messy.

But Jesus is off the cross, out of the grave, and running wild in the world.

RIFFING ON RESURRECTION

- How is God drawing you toward grace and peace in your mess right now?
- Where in your life does God want to do a work of resurrection?

2.2

JESUS, CENTER STAGE

Immense in mercy and with an incredible love, he embraced us.
He took our sin-dead lives and made us alive in Christ.

EPHESIANS 2:4-5

Listen: This is the gospel. The best possible news. Write this down. Make it the epitaph on your gravestone. Tattoo it on your arm (unless of course, you think that kind of stuff is bad, bad, bad—then ignore that suggestion). Memorize it. Pitch in with your buddies to hire a skywriter. Post it online. Tell it with a joyful smile to the next person who asks you what this whole Christianity thing is about.

Jesus makes dead people alive.

Let that soak in for a minute. Close this book for the day—I won't mind; I'll still be here waiting for you tomorrow. Go live your life, and while you do, let this truth blow your mind.

The good news is not that Jesus makes bad people good.

The good news is not that Jesus makes decent, moral people even better.

The good news is not that Jesus takes rebels and failures and does an extreme makeover on them.

None of that.

The good news is that Jesus makes dead people alive.

The Bible tells us that when we were trapped in our sin, we were *dead*. This is binary stuff: dead and alive. You don't get *less* dead—you get *un*dead.[1]

At one point you are dead, and at the next moment you are alive. How? Who flips that switch?

God does. Father, Son, and Spirit. The Bible tells us that God is overflowing with mercy because of his measureless love for us. Look how Ephesians 2:4 (ESV) starts: "But God . . ."

Okay, pause here for a minute. Because it's all about God, right? Everything starts and finishes with God.

"But God, being rich in mercy, because of the great love with which he loved us, even when we were dead in our trespasses . . ." (Ephesians 2:4-5, ESV).

And stop right there. Because whatever happens next, it's going to be the best thing ever, right? Rich mercy and great love—even when we deserved neither!

---

[1] Well, not undead like a zombie is undead. I mean *not* dead.

". . . made us alive together with Christ" (v. 5, ESV).

That's everything, right there. That crazy "John 3:16" banner guy in the end zone has got it right. Because God loved people *so* much, God sent his willing Son, Jesus, to become a human—one of us! And now *anyone* who follows Jesus, who puts Jesus in charge of his or her life—*that person's life will never come to an end, but will continue on into God's perfect and joyous eternity.*

And it gets even better: This plan wasn't hatched to get us in trouble or beat us down. Rather, as John 3:17 tells us, the entire purpose of God's plan isn't to condemn the world . . . it's to *save the world*, through Jesus.

Without Jesus, we're dead.

Perhaps we are good without Jesus. Responsible. Successful. Upright and decent and admired. Perhaps we are reviled. Hated, even. But none of that matters if we're not in relationship with Jesus.

Without Jesus, no matter who we are, we're dead—and the moment we choose God, the switch gets flipped.

Off / On

Dead / Alive

I love how the Bible paints the picture: We're trapped in the kingdom of darkness, and Jesus is the only one with the power to ride into that kingdom, to subdue our evil captor, and to rescue us, taking us back into the Kingdom of light. Forever. *No one* can be snatched away from God.

Kingdom of Darkness / Kingdom of Light. Forever. Boom!

Let me say one more thing about this, the best of all

possible good news. Remember how the bad news is worse than we realize? That we're rebels and failures who will never, no matter how hard we try, make it out of the messiness? That's exactly why the good news is all the sweeter. Infinitely sweet. Because God looks at us, just as we are, and says, "I am merciful. I love you with an everlasting love. And I will put back together what is broken."

It's one thing to embrace a decent person. A grateful person. But it's a different deal entirely to embrace a hideous person. A bitter person. A person who is *actively* rebelling against your love.

This reminds me of a guy God used in my life in a serious way. Larry did campus ministry even though he was older and had bright-white hair and did *not* look the part for connecting with kids. But every time I saw Larry, he was so kind, and joyful, and genuinely interested in what I was doing. Every time he would ask a probing question, he knew when to back off when I got aggressive or to press when I engaged. Larry would invite me to hang and never looked dejected when I turned him down. Just a wide-open door. He hung in there with me when I was stoned and arrogant and angry and unintelligibly patronizing. He loved me just as I was and didn't judge me for what I wasn't.

I'll never forget when my mother died, Larry came to the wake and the funeral service. I shared my mom's eulogy. That was the first time I ever stood in a pulpit. After we left the church, Larry stood off at a distance and waited until I got a million hugs and kisses from friends and family. He just stood there, smiling, but not the type of smile that would have been awkward at a funeral. It was what I know now as "the peace of God which surpasses all understanding" smile, the smile of a person who knows that he is beloved of God. At the time, I caught his eye after every few interactions, and he waited for close to an hour. Finally, with that gentle smile, he swung his arm around me and said, "How are you doing, brother?" And I cried. Like sobbing and messy. And he simply hugged me, in all my pain and garbage.

What's cool is that I still connect with Larry to this day— but now we are brothers! That kind of welcome is exactly what God does for us. While you were *still* a sinner, the Bible says, Jesus chose to die for you, to save you. While *I* was still a sinner, Jesus died for me.

Honestly? I sin every single stinking day. I'm a sinner. And God says to us—to me, the pastor and dad and husband who just keeps sinning and sinning—"I have mercy and great love for you."

For some of you reading right now, God put this book in your hands specifically so that you could hear this. It's something you've never heard, and it's literally going to change your life.

God does not love you because you're good; God loves you because God is loving.

And God sees you in *all* of your brokenness, in *all* of your messiness, in *all* of your sin, and God embraces you with overflowing compassion and transforming love. As many have phrased it, there is nothing you can do that will make

God love you more . . . *and there is nothing you can do that will make God love you less.*

Is that a God worth following? Worth trusting and worshiping?

Without Jesus, you're dead. With Jesus, you're alive. That's what it means to be a Christian.

Dead / Alive

Once you're illuminated, once you're shining, there's no snuffing you out. There's no going back. And that's the reason we work to follow Jesus, to build God's Kingdom, to listen to the Spirit's sometimes uncomfortable prompting.

Because when Jesus saves your life, you can't imagine doing anything else.

RIFFING ON THE SWITCH

- What is your honest response to this statement? *God does not love you because you're good; God loves you because God is loving.*
- If you're following Jesus, do you sense that you have been changed from dead to alive? Why or why not?

2.3

SAVED

It's in Christ that you, once you heard the truth and believed it (this Message of your salvation), found yourselves home free—signed, sealed, and delivered by the Holy Spirit.

EPHESIANS 1:14

This good news, it sounds great, right? A little *too* great, in fact—too good to be true!

Guess what? It *is* too good to be true!

But it's still true.

So why in the world does Jesus save us? Why bother with us at all?

I'll tell you one thing: It isn't so that you and I can start working hard to be good, just so we can sort of "prove" to God that we "deserved" to be saved. Like, *Don't worry, God, you made the right call by saving me! You don't have to have second thoughts about your plan to send Jesus to die for me and make me alive . . . I'm totally worth it!*

It sounds bad to say it like that, but don't we often make assumptions along those lines? We get a little too comfortable with the narrative, and so we leap to unwarranted conclusions. The whole deal is a head-scratcher. It just doesn't make sense for God to go to such painful, extravagant lengths to save such unlovable creatures as us.

Unless we're actually worth saving.

Unless we're lovable.

Unless we're important.

Otherwise, *why bother?*

I'm here to tell you, those are not the primary reasons that God is saving you. Jesus entered the messiness of human life, and God sent the Spirit into the messiness of life, for another reason—a reason that includes you, yes, but goes beyond you and carries you into something unimaginably greater.

Throughout the Bible, the message of Jesus, the coming

of Jesus, the reality of how life can now be lived *because* of Jesus—all that is called "good news." And it's good news for all people, all nations, all societies, and not just for the awesome individuals who are "worth" saving. The reason this sort of far-reaching news is *good* is that God knows some important things about what it's like to be a human.

Actually God knows *exactly* what it's like to be a human. And not just because he created us. Since Jesus became a human and was tempted in *every way, just like we are*, God knows what daily life is like for us. God knows what it's like to live with messiness.

So God knows all too well that our relationship with him is broken.

That our relationship with ourselves is broken because our relationship with God is broken.

And that as a consequence, our relationships with others are broken.

What did Jesus come to do? Let's hear it in Jesus' own words, quoting the prophet Isaiah:

> The Spirit of the Lord is upon Me,
> Because He anointed Me to preach the gospel to
>   the poor.
> He has sent Me to proclaim release to the captives,
> And recovery of sight to the blind,
> To set free those who are oppressed,
> To proclaim the favorable year of the Lord.
>
> LUKE 4:18-19, NASB

In other words, to restore broken relationships. God is not content to leave us down in the dumps, whether getting there was our fault or not.

God accepts us just as we are but loves us too much to let us stay that way. Instead, God is reconciling *all* our relationships, with grace and peace. Remember, the Hebrew word for "peace" is *shalom,* which means wholeness and restoration.

So when we're in pieces, the only solution is God's peace, made possible only by God's grace.

This is the paradox of being human. We're more broken than we want to admit, but God's love is even greater than our brokenness. So we're neither self-exalting *nor* self-deprecating. Instead, we're children of God—normal folks who once were dead, yet now are alive. We're Lazarus.

That is the radical realism of the Bible.

As we follow Jesus and listen to what God is telling us—through the Bible, other people's wise counsel, the desires of our hearts, and his Spirit—we start to discover things in our heart that shouldn't be there.

"Yup, that's not helpful. You're right, God: I do that, and I don't want to. I see that it's not based in love or kindness or peacemaking. It's my own garbage, my own attempts at self-preservation. Please help me."

God rejoices in and honors that. God works in us and with us. We'll never be perfect, but we can become more like that tree from Psalm 1, planted by streams of water, that bears fruit in season: love, joy, peace, patience, kindness, goodness, faithfulness, gentleness, self-control. That's a lifelong transformation, which is why we love to say at our church, *we are all in process.*

But we're also saved—and we're who God chooses to be the body of Christ in the world. We're God's people, the church, and we're living messages of restoration and wholeness.

RIFFING ON SALVATION

- How does knowing that God desires to save people change how *we* view people?
- What fruit is God developing in your life? What is he revealing to you about where you are in process?

2.4

LIVING GOD-STYLE

The mystery is that people who have never heard of God and those who have heard of him all their lives (what I've been calling outsiders and insiders) stand on the same ground before God. They get the same offer, same help, same promises in Christ Jesus. The Message is accessible and welcoming to everyone, across the board. . . . When we trust in him, we're free to say whatever needs to be said, bold to go wherever we need to go.

EPHESIANS 3:5-6, 12

The good news of the Christian message—if we follow it, if we follow Jesus—takes us outside of ourselves. That's the beauty of it. That it's not about us.

And yet it *is* about us as well—just not about us as anything ultimate or preeminent. Because doesn't that get old, really fast? I don't know about you, but honestly, I get sick of myself. I want to be divorced from my self-obsession. I want something better. Something bigger.

Something not invented for self-preservation by a rebel and a failure.

When it's about us, we end up with our heads stuck up our proverbial you-know-whats *way* too often.

"I'll do X, Y, and Z. I'll raise my kids well. I'll be an example at my job."

And if we do those things, we say, "Hooray, I'm a good Christian now!"

I hate to break it to you. (I hate to break it to *me*!) You're not a good Christian because you did *any* of that! *None* of it makes you a better Christian.

So what *does* make you a good Christian person?

The fact that Jesus is the Christ.

See, the good things we do are just that: good. Good, but not ultimate. They can't save. Giving money to your church, or a charity? That's *good*—but it can't *save* anyone. Same goes for church attendance, fasting, community volunteer days, and whatever other criteria we come up with.

At the end of the day, and at the end of time, it's not about what you've done or left undone—it's about what Jesus has done for you, and whether you've accepted that gift. That's why the finished work of Jesus' cross makes the playing field completely level, because *anyone* can accept the gift of Jesus.

That's one of the things that I love so much about my family of faith at Crossroads Community Church. There are all sorts of people there. At each one of our gatherings, we set aside time to share God's love with one another. It is so cool to see the diversity of the body of Christ. Tatted-up bikers hugging sweet older ladies. Lifelong Christians talking with brand-new believers. Seekers and nonbelievers welcomed. Eyes that tell the story of both suffering and joy. And all of us mixing together into a wild, Jesus-shaped family! The Bible tells us that *all people* have equal access to God, through Jesus, *and we all need Jesus just as much as anyone else.*

There's this beautiful passage, Ephesians 2:11-13, where Paul is like, "But now, in Jesus, all of you who used to be *outside* God's house have been invited *inside*—because of what Jesus did on the cross!" (author's paraphrase).

The Cross is the great leveler. The ultimate democratizer. Smasher of human-created barriers and boundaries. There is *no* human distinction that can keep us outside of God's house, so long as our invitation is what Jesus did for us.

Isn't that crazy? Like, no bouncers or guest lists or busybodies at God's place, ever. Instead, Jesus gives us access to God the Father. The Bible tells us that *through* Jesus, and *in* God's Spirit, we have access to, you know, *God* . . . the One who created every single one of the hundred-octillion stars in the universe! Here the word *access* literally means to make an introduction between two people, so they can get to know each other.

Think of going to the White House, and actually being invited in for a chat, rather than wrestled to the ground by some Secret Service guy and his slobbery German shepherd.

That access to God can change everything for us. I know it did in my life. Before I started following Jesus and continuing afterward, I was playing the electric and upright bass like crazy—and I was getting crazy good! (I say that in true humility, okay? Humility isn't putting yourself down all the time. Humility is being honest about your weaknesses *and* your strengths. I'll freely admit, running is not one of my strengths. On the flip side, though, the bass *is* one of my strengths.) I spent time making a living as a professional bass player, and since bass is the bacon of music and everyone follows the bass player, I was a made man. If I hadn't responded to Jesus' call into the ministry, I would probably still be playing professionally today. That's just me being honest, and putting my strengths *and* my weaknesses out there.[2]

Anyway, I was thinking something along these lines:

Yeah man, I'm gonna be on the cover of Bass Player *magazine, you know? Just looking awesome while I'm holding out my bass like a* boss! *I'll be on the road, selling out concerts and putting out albums. I'll be* doin' *it!*

When God heard that, he said, "Daniel, I know that you love the bass, and I've given you the gift to be awesome at it! But—no, listen, listen, seriously, *listen*—I've created you for something more."

That was painful to hear at first. But slowly the truth soaked in: that I was making music my identity. I was making my gift about me. I was focused on the gift and was

---

[2] To be safe, here are four more of my weaknesses: shaving, handwriting, not eating everything I can find, and—according to my bride, Lynn—keeping my feet to myself. Just saying.)

neglecting the gift-giver. That's not why God gives us gifts, though. Not just for us.

God gives us gifts so that we can be part of something bigger! And once I stopped playing the bass for myself, for my own identity, and started playing it for God, and for others, I discovered something: *I'd never enjoyed playing the bass more.*

I was aiming at a self-styled life, but God gave me a God-styled life. Guess which one is better?

Now on stage at church, when I'm worshiping, I can just hit that note, and even if Jason, our music pastor who happens to have perfect pitch, gives me the stink-eye, *it doesn't matter.* Know why?

Because Jesus died and came alive, and Jesus knows I'm full of wrong notes.

So every time I hit a wrong note during worship, and Jason's eye-of-Sauron catches my gaze, and a vein throbs on his neck, I'm like, "That's because I believe in the gospel!" Ba-*dowww.* Ba-*dowww.* I'll play that wrong note again and again and again. Ba-*dowww.*

I'm *full* of wrong notes! And Jesus loves me!

And guess what? You're full of wrong notes too. We're all full of wrong notes together, living God-style in the midst of this world. And he's created all of us for something bigger.

RIFFING ON ACCESS

- God has given all of us equal access to himself. How does knowing this change the way you see the people around you?

- What gifts has God given you? How do you sense him calling you to use those gifts for his bigger purposes?

2.5

SCHOOLING ANGELS

Through followers of Jesus like yourselves gathered in churches, this extraordinary plan of God is becoming known and talked about even among the angels!

EPHESIANS 3:10

Ready for something crazy? I don't mean normal-crazy, either. Like when my wife tells me that a new pizza joint opened up nearby, and I go, "What? *Crazy!*"

I'm talking about actual-crazy. Like, doesn't-make-sense-at-all-and-no-sane-person-would-dare-to-invent-it crazy. Here we go. I'm just going to say it, straight out.

The church is God's way of schooling angels.

I know, I know, that sounds nuts. I grew up in a northeast Italian family, nominally Catholic, where going to church was like, "Oh man, do we have to? That place is so boring!" In fact, the only thing I liked about church, when we occasionally went, was that the pew had this curved, wooden edge to it, and it was *perfect* for practicing my bass scales. I'd sit there, tapping my toe, and flicking my fingers through scale after scale—major scale modes, arpeggios, even chromatic runs when the homily was especially perplexing—until my mom inevitably caught on and gave my hand a quick slap with the bulletin.

So the first time I read this concept, I did a double take. Here's the way Paul puts it in the third chapter of Ephesians: "[God's] intent was that now, through the church, the manifold wisdom of God should be made known to the rulers and authorities in the heavenly realms, according to his eternal purpose that he accomplished in Christ Jesus our Lord" (verses 10-11, NIV).

That's a mouthful. But you read it, and think about what's actually being said, and if you're anything like me, you go, "Wait, so the *angels* are looking at the church and being wowed by God's wisdom? We must be talking about some *other* church!"

For a lot of us, the grass is always greener, so to speak, when it comes to churches. And I won't deny that some churches do some things better than others—that's a biblical concept. But we're not talking about *the church you go to or I go to* here . . . we're talking about the universal, global, generation-after-generation church. Not a building, but a people. The people of God!

And this is why church is such a big deal.

The church is a shining, galactic testimony to God's wisdom and loving purpose: that in Jesus, *all humans can enjoy restored relationships with God and with each other.*

This is where our twenty-first-century culture and following Jesus separate. It's common for people to say, "I like Jesus, just not the church." In God's view, though, that statement doesn't hold water. Find a living, healthy, joyful church, by all means! But the call for followers of Jesus to be part of a community of faith is not a gray area in the Bible. It isn't some optional part of Christianity people can agree to disagree on. It's fundamental and foundational. *God intends his children to live in community and relationship as the body of Christ.*

We are not called to *go* to church but to perpetually *be* the church. We're *all* called into something bigger and greater—something with Jesus at its head and people from every country and race and gender and economic level and political party and age and personality type surrounding us. I'm a tiny, finite human, and the scale of God's ambition absolutely shocks me!

Psychologists use the term *gestalt theory* for this idea that the whole is bigger and greater than the individual parts. A set of brakes is good, but brakes are even better when they're part of a car. A first baseman is great,[3] but he's even better when he's part of a baseball team.

Same with you. Same with me. We're designed to be part of something greater, something bigger, something more beautiful than any individual could ever be alone.

That's more good news, more of the gospel right there: You were made alive and saved by God to be part of this living, organic experience called "church." And the church is not a building of bricks and mortar—it's a building of people.

People who've committed every single sin in the book.

People redeemed by Jesus.

---

[3] Unless he plays for the Dodgers, because when you leave Brooklyn, fuggetaboutit.

People in process, who have been changed and are being changed by the grace of God.

People led by the Spirit.

That's church. *That's* why God saves us, and *that's* the church the angels are looking at, and the angelic equivalents of minds are just getting *blown*!

So the next time you're tempted to put down the church, and criticize all its mistakes, remember that the church is the textbook, the curriculum, that God uses to teach the angels. It's indispensable! It's a privilege to be part of!

You might be thinking, *Okay, the church is deeper than I thought. I get the angel thing. But still, it's not for me, you know? I don't want in. I don't need in.*

Here's the challenge I'm going to leave you with. Try to find *any* other organization or group—and bonus points if it's existed for a few thousand years—in which you can find people of *every* single background, every single . . . *everything*—who nevertheless are part of the same organism. United in the same purpose. Encouraging, bearing one another's burdens, growing in the fruit of God's Spirit, taking those gifts into the world, and giving thanks to the Giver.

Look, I know that church is messy. And the universal church isn't always pretty. The Bible tells us that the church is a bride preparing for her wedding day—and sometimes church can be bridezilla! But honestly, church is God's brilliance in action. Don't let the cynics convince you that the church has ruined the world—the truth is quite the opposite! It's easy to rock the boat, but a lot harder to row it across the lake.

My recommendation is that when it comes to church, be part of the solution, not part of the problem. Learn to live "full in the fullness of God. God can do anything, you know—far more than you could ever imagine or guess or request in your wildest dreams!" (Ephesians 3:19-20).

RIFFING ON ANGELS

- What struggles do you have with the church?
- Do you see yourself as a part of the universal church? How is God calling you to be a part of his *solution*?

2.6

FAR MORE THAN YOU COULD EVER IMAGINE

I ask him to strengthen you by his Spirit—not a brute strength but a glorious inner strength—that Christ will live in you as you open the door and invite him in. And I ask him that with both feet planted firmly on love, you'll be able to take in with all followers of Jesus the extravagant dimensions of Christ's love. Reach out and experience the breadth! Test its length! Plumb the depths! Rise to the heights! Live full lives, full in the fullness of God. God can do anything, you know—far more than you could ever imagine or guess or request in your wildest dreams!

EPHESIANS 3:14-20

When we're made alive and saved and brought into this crazy thing called the church where we live God-style . . . well, then we get stuff *done!* Following Jesus, and being empowered by the Spirit, gives us the ability to endure, to overcome, to accomplish amazing things.

Everyone wants to have the ability to effect things. We want the capacity to reshape or create the world around us as we desire. The power to make things right.

But the truth of it is, we can't make the messiness of this world right, no matter how hard we try.

But someone else can.

There are some things that only Jesus can do. Because when it comes to power, it's Jesus who has all of it, always!

Jesus has cornered the market on power. We think we have power, we think others have power, but in reality, Jesus has it all. Say we have the power to make a certain decision. Even that is us being asked to administer Jesus' power here on earth. How do I know? Check out what Jesus says about himself at the very end of Matthew's gospel.

All authority in heaven and on earth has been given
to me.
MATTHEW 28:18, NIV

Not a lot of wiggle room there. And this isn't the only place we're told this. There's an image the writers of the New Testament use over and over, and it backs up Jesus' claim. *All things*, we're told, *are under the feet of Jesus.* We aren't into images like that these days. It sounds barbaric, or even cruel, right? We'd rather have Jesus hugging and high-fiving everyone. We're uncomfortable with the image of Jesus as some sort of street fighter, stepping on the neck of his beaten opponent. Or a conqueror crushing everything in his path.

Unless. Unless what he's fighting and crushing *deserves* it. See, God's kids are safe from that warrior Jesus, that all-authority-in-heaven-and-earth Jesus. Completely safe! But you know what isn't?

Evil.

And that's more good news. Don't we *want* Jesus to step on some necks and do some crushing? Think about it. Some of the messiness in your life you can handle. Some of it isn't really that big of a deal. Like in ten years, you aren't going to remember that guy who cut you off while driving, just like you aren't going to remember who unfriended you on Facebook. That kind of messiness is small potatoes.

But friend, some of the messiness of life is *pure evil*, plain and simple. I don't have to list any examples because you feel them in your gut, and we have all seen that evil in action. They're the things that are so *wrong* that you can't stand them. The things that make you shiver with fear, or scream, or want to curl up into a ball and weep.

It may not be kosher to say stuff like this, but I can't *wait* for the day that Jesus absolutely rips evil a new one. Kicks it to the curb and then keeps on kicking, until the face of evil is a bloody mess. I want Jesus to give evil what it's got coming! To straight *destroy* it! Because until evil is completely defeated, we cannot be completely free of the real mess, and we cannot be completely healed, whole, and joyful.

And *everything* points to this trajectory—the Bible, nature, experience, history, the testimony of saints who have gone before us, the longing in our hearts that sometimes we don't even admit to ourselves—that there is meant to be a final end to evil and a beginning of endless joy.

Here's the wild thing about Jesus, one of the things that makes Jesus God and us us.

Jesus teaches the universe how ultimate power is ultimately meant to be used.

You've heard, "Power tends to corrupt and absolute power corrupts absolutely."[4] That's always true with us humans, but never true with Jesus. Jesus has absolute power, and he uses it for absolute justice and goodness. He promised us, and he's got the power to see it through to the end. Read Revelation 19 if you don't believe me, and Colossians 1:15-20, and about every fourth psalm.

No matter what you believe about the end times or heaven, what *every* Christian can agree on is this: Jesus is going to set things right, back to how God designed them to be. There will be full shalom, real peace, that none of us have *ever* fully experienced. And when that comes to pass, there will be no more pain or tears or evil. None. Read Revelation 21:1-4.

There is a "joy beyond the walls of the world," as Tolkien puts it,[5] a place where there is unending life beyond this life. It will be in *that* life, through the powerful love and loving power of Jesus, that messiness will meet its match forever.

---

[4] Lord Acton, letter to Archbishop Mandell Creighton, April 5, 1877, http://history.hanover.edu/courses/excerpts/165acton.html (accessed July 14, 2015).
[5] J. R. R. Tolkien, *The Tolkien Reader* (New York: Ballantine Books, 1966), 68.

RIFFING ON POWER

- How do you feel knowing that Jesus has all the power?
- How does the reality that Jesus has power to ultimately triumph over the mess change things in the present?

CODA

Honestly, the mess never goes away. It just doesn't. But here's what Jesus means for you. Right now, today, in the midst of your mess.

Jesus is a gift for the mess. The presence of Jesus is our present in the mess.

Not a golden ticket out of the mess, but a gift within the mess.

This isn't about pie-in-the-sky escapism. Christians sometimes get knocked for being so heavenly minded that we're no earthly good. But Jesus wants to share the life of God with us, starting now. God *knows* what it's like to be a soul in a body, with every longing and temptation and desire and need our bodies produce. God became human. Literally human. And part of the reason was to teach us how to walk.

We all have to walk through the mess. You do, I do. That's what the next section is about: that there really isn't an alternative.

Life *is* walking through the mess.

But.

But instead of walking through the mess alone, you can walk through it with Jesus.

That may sound trivial. It isn't. Not even close.

Let that marinate for a moment. You get to walk through your life with Jesus.

Jesus created the world. Then became part of that world—a messy human just like you and me. Yet he lived perfectly before God and people. Yet he allowed himself to be killed. Then was raised back to everlasting life by God's power—and he didn't stop there. Ephesians 1:21-22 tells us that God "set him on a throne in deep heaven, in charge of running the universe, everything from galaxies to governments, no name and no power exempt from his rule. And not just for the time being, but *forever*. He is in charge of it all, has the final word on everything."

And *that's* the person you have walking with you, through the mess.

That means everything. That *changes* everything.

We can't escape the mess. The messiness of life is the real deal.

But Jesus is the realer deal, and he won't let *us* escape *him*. Because he's the one who can do "far more than you could ever imagine or guess or request in your wildest dreams!"

Including making dead people alive.

Alive *forever*.

And alive *now*, even as we walk through this life.

PART III
PURSUANCE

YOU HAVE TO GO THROUGH IT

In light of all this, here's what I want you to do. While I'm locked up here, a prisoner for the Master, I want you to get out there and walk—better yet, run!—on the road God called you to travel. I don't want any of you sitting around on your hands. I don't want anyone strolling off, down some path that goes nowhere.

EPHESIANS 4:1-2

Here's an honest, though depressing, thought: Life would actually be *less* messy if I didn't exist.

Even if you don't know me in real life, by this point in the book you know that's the truth. I've got issues. I make mistakes and bad choices. I've told you about a bunch of them already, so no need to summarize them here, right?[1] So part of the messiness of life is my fault. I contribute to it—both to my own mess and to the general messiness of the world.

Or that *would* be depressing, if not for Jesus. Because it's the grace and peace provided by Jesus that are the remedy for the mess. Life is messy, yes, but Jesus *is* real. Jesus rules over the mess and works in and through the mess, whether that mess is "out there" or "in here"—outside in our worlds or inside our hearts. Jesus is not afraid of it, nor is Jesus ignorant of it. Actually, Jesus is *Lord* of it. So while life *would* be less messy if I didn't exist, if I didn't exist there would be one

---

[1] Just to be *extra* safe, though, here are four more ways I add to the messiness of life: thoughtlessly making jokes that hurt people, not calling my extended family often enough, not following Jesus' Greatest Commandment passionately enough, and continuing to root for the New York Knicks in basketball.

less person to follow Jesus through the mess, day in and day out. When people do that, God has a chance to shine in our lives, and then *we* shine, glowing like a light in the darkness because of God's grace.

Did you catch that? *We get to follow Jesus through the mess.*

We can't go *around* the mess because the mess is everywhere: relationships, jobs, hobbies, churches, governments, nature, school. If we're human, we live *in* the mess, and if we're alive, we live *through* the mess. Because not living *in* the mess means escaping humanity, and not living *through* the mess means ending life right now. Living in and through is our only option.

But *how?*

That's not just a fair question—it's an essential question. In one form or another, folks have been asking that since we started asking questions. What's the best way to live? And even if we know, can we actually *do* it? Even the anguished cry of "why?" is a form of this question, because it hinges on an inability to understand why the "rules" of life have apparently been broken.

You work hard at your job, but you get fired anyway by a corrupt manager.

You save your money, but an unexpected medical expense bankrupts you.

You toss out a thoughtless joke to a friend, and the friendship never recovers.

You pray to God for wisdom, and the big decision you make turns out disastrously.

Why?

Why, in other words, did life stop working the way you thought it was meant to work? Unless you're contemplating suicide, the *why* is inextricably linked to the *how*.[2] And if life is really this messy, how are we meant to live from here on out?

God's design for followers of Jesus is that they walk through the mess in a very specific way. A lot like a bass line in jazz, there is a specific way, a rhythm and flow, an appropriateness to our choice of notes. For much of the tune, the bass player, along with the drummer, is providing the foundation on which the other players can build their parts, from piano to saxophone or whatever instruments are involved. As we walk the bass line of our lives, we either create a context in which others around us can flourish, or we detract from their opportunity to do that.

And human flourishing is exactly what God is after. Listen to Jesus: "I have come that they may have life, and have it to the full" (John 10:10, NIV). Some translations have "to the full" as "more abundantly." Think about that. God doesn't want us to be stuck in a rut—God wants us to be free to flourish, and more! Just like jazz, one of the coolest things about God is that we aren't confined by a single set of notes. God is infinitely creative. And so not only is each person called to be part of a unique tune, God is able to adapt and improvise the tune of each person's life.

---

2 And if you are contemplating suicide, put down this book right now and call 1-800-273-8255. It's a free, confidential line that will hook you up with a wise and caring person who can listen to you and help you. Please don't wait.

So let's look at how God wants us to walk through the mess. How are we meant to live in such a way that God is glorified and others have the chance to flourish?

RIFFING ON WALKING

- How can you become more aware of Jesus walking with you through the mess?
- What does your flourishing life in Jesus actually look like?

3.2

WALK THIS WAY

You were all called to travel on the same road and in the same direction, so stay together, both outwardly and inwardly. You have one Master, one faith, one baptism, one God and Father of all, who rules over all, works through all, and is present in all. Everything you are and think and do is permeated with Oneness.

EPHESIANS 4:4-6

Each one of us—you, me, that weirdo at work who you always try to avoid, whoever—*all* of us are called by Jesus to walk a certain way. With every breath, with every beat of our hearts, every single moment, we're called by Jesus to walk with him, the way *he* walks.

Jesus is calling us, and the thing about calling is that it transcends circumstances. It doesn't depend on whether we're up or down, good or bad, rich or poor. It's like if our heart is beating, Jesus wants it to be beating in time with *his* heart, no matter what we're doing. And that's the rhythm to which we walk through the mess.

God has a *design* for us, as followers of Jesus, for how to walk through life. Ask any musician what would happen if every member of the band started playing a different genre simultaneously! Any composer or bandleader has a plan for how the musicians are going to interact, for the benefit of the music. So there is meant to be an appropriateness to the notes we choose to play with our lives—to the notes we are *called* or *invited* to play with our lives.

Here's an example that I'm 99 percent positive will be worth it—because it's about the bass, and if you haven't picked up on it by now, I love me some bass!

For some reason, people always seem to be clamoring for a bass player. After I picked up my first upright bass in college, I started to get requests to play various gigs. Not saying the invitations were to play at sweet venues. The gigs ranged from smoky bars to stuffy restaurants where they set the band up behind a row of fake plants. But still. I was on a gig!

So there I was, trying to figure out how to play this monstrosity of an instrument, which was taller than me and made my fingers bleed. I dragged it over to the Mason Gross School of the Arts at Rutgers, and I pretty much begged—I'd like to say charmed, but I can't—my way into a bunch of classes and combos. You've seen that movie *Rudy*, where Sam Gamgee walks on to the Notre Dame football team, and even though he stinks and is too small, he has a bottomless heart and endless desire and he ends up being an on-the-field hero? I was the Rudy of bass players!

Eventually I ended up getting to take private lessons with virtuoso bass player Ken Filiano. He could play anything—classical, bow or no bow, jazz, you name it—but when it came to what most would call avant-garde or creative music, that dude could throw *down*.[3] I couldn't get enough of that stuff, and Ken was just a monster at playing it. Studying with Maestro Filiano was a revelation. He pulled sounds out of the bass that were unlike anything I'd ever heard. I'd stand there, geeking out as he played, and then I couldn't wait to get on *my* bass and try to get it to make a *fraction* of the sounds he'd been making. I'd go to a practice room and just play play play, as hard as I could, bloody fingers and all. I started to figure out some stuff that was straight *weird*. And I loved it.

Tiny problem: I had no idea how to actually play the bass in its established role. Although Ken was trying hard to make sure I knew the conventional stuff, I was only truly interested in the way-out-there stuff. Crazy, avant-garde artist in training? Totally had that down. But supporting the rest of the band with a steady rhythm and by outlining the chords? Not so much.

Which is why I was also fortunate, and frustrated, that I was in jazz combos with Larry Ridley, a bass player who had tons of album credits under his belt. And he forced

---

[3]My wife isn't one who would call it avant-garde or creative, by the way. She prefers to call it "noise" or "Daniel jazz." I love you, honey!

me—harassed me—into playing the "right lines" and playing "the changes" and all the rest. We'd face each other in the studio and he'd fight with me to play these classic walking bass lines. Me watching him watching me, every note right on cue, right on the supporting chord. It was all about supporting the music from the background—about stepping out of the spotlight and making other people sound better. And he was right: Just like I had no real idea how to play avant-garde "noise," I also was unable to play conventional bass.

I tell you all this because what I didn't know at the time[4] was that the bass isn't a single, unified instrument with a single, unified purpose. Like, I thought I wanted to learn how to "play the bass," but that's sort of like saying, "I want to learn how to speak language!" Which language? For what purpose? How fluently?

There's a sports personality named Bill Simmons. He's on the television now, but I loved it when he was just a writer. He's hilarious because he relates almost everything to movies and bands from the 1980s. He's coined a few phrases, like "The Tyson Zone," which describes celebrities who could do literally anything and you wouldn't be surprised.

So Simmons came up with a concept that basically covers a lot of biblical ground, though I can't guarantee he's aware of his influences. It's called "Christian years" for athletes, and here's how it works. Think about Mariano Rivera, who

---

[4] I'm going to cut my younger self some slack. I was twenty—of *course* I didn't know this at the time! And if you know and love a twenty-year-old? Cut 'em some slack too. They'll grow on you, literally. And if *you're* the twenty-year-old? Just keep doing what you're doing, and life and grace and time will take care of the rest, God willing.

recently retired from the New York Yankees at age forty-three as the best closer in baseball history and was still pitching like a player half his age. And on the other hand, you've got a guy like Dennis Rodman, the former basketball player, who hasn't honored Jesus with his body, and when he was forty-three he looked freakishly aged already. So you compare these two elite athletes, at similar points in life, and you want to know why they're *so* different. The answer is Christian years. Bill Simmons would remind people that sure, Rivera was technically post-forty, but he's post-forty in Christian years. As opposed to party years, drug years, sleeping-three-hours-a-night years.

If a secular sports writer gets it, we can get it. *The way we walk matters.*

God is calling us to walk a certain way, through the mess. He's calling us to learn how to play our bass in its established role. And for a good reason! God isn't calling us to just "live our lives"—God is calling us to live in a specific way, for the purpose of his glory and our ultimate happiness.

Check out what Paul writes about us in Ephesians 2:10: "For we are God's masterpiece. He has created us anew in Christ Jesus, so we can do the good things he planned for us long ago" (NLT).

Wait, what? *What?*

It's true! Before we were even born, God made a plan to save us—thank you, Jesus!—*so that we could do the good things he already has planned for us!* That's why our walk is vital. The rhythm of our actions has to match God's music.

RIFFING ON DESIGN

- What good works have you seen God plan out for you so far?
- How would your life look different if you were walking the way Jesus walks?

3.3

GETTING INTIMATE

My response is to get down on my knees before the Father.

EPHESIANS 3:14

Here's the thing, though. Following the rhythm of God's music doesn't just happen. Walking with him through the mess takes conversation and relationship. Want to know what we call that conversation and relationship?

Prayer. And like any relationship, it grows by communication over time. That's a great definition of intimacy—communication over time—and people with the most intimate relationship with God are people who have prayed the most. Talked to God the most, and listened in return.

But also like any relationship, and like life itself, prayer is messy. Sometimes it can seem so messy that it isn't even worth our trouble. How does it work? How should we do it? Why should we do it? How do we know if a prayer will be answered, and what should we do if it isn't?

Life is messy in different ways for us, but the reality is

that we'd all like to be able to pray for something and get it. Wouldn't it be great to un-mess our lives by just asking God for whatever we need? Some of us want our illness to go away. Some of us want to pay our heating bill. Some of us want to meet a companion so we won't be alone. Most of the things we want are actually good things too!

Right now, even while you're reading this, you can think of something you want. Something that feels like it would make all the difference. But you're not sure prayer is the way to get it.

We've all experienced it—asking God for something and not receiving it. We wonder what's the point of prayer, anyway.

Here's what's causing the disconnect: When we pray, we often want the benefits without the costs.

That might sound harsh, but it's true. We want God's provision without the process, or the gift without the lesson that teaches it.

We'd never dream of doing that in a "real" relationship. In fact, that is a marker of what kind of a relationship we're in. Think of your friend who keeps dating and dating without settling down. Everyone but him knows the problem: He only gets into relationships for one person—himself. Take, take, take. When the costs start rising, like when his latest girlfriend is dealing with some health issues, he bails.

Now I'm no paragon of relationship wisdom, but at the very least I *am* in a real relationship. I've been married to my wife for more than ten years, going on forever, and we're as happy together as two messy people can be. I know something about what relationships cost. Like I would never come home and start demanding things from my wife. *Give me dinner, massage my shoulders, and tell me how wonderful I am—and make the kids sit calmly at my feet and brush the dog's teeth.* Yeah, that would *never* work.

Actually, let me be honest: It *would* totally work.

But only for a while, right? My wife would attempt to do that, but only because we have an established, give-and-take relationship. We have a history. We trust each other. We work for each other and love each other. So the first time I did that, she'd assume I had a good reason, and she'd give it a shot. Just like I would for her if she demanded something.

Or maybe I should put the word "work" in quotes. Because I'd be burning through relational capital faster than Snoop Dogg through blunts or the New York Yankees through free agents or James Bond through beautiful women or the Cookie Monster through, well, cookies!

So it might work for me to demand all those benefits, but only in the sense that it would *happen.* It wouldn't be sustainable. It wouldn't be ongoing. We all know relationships can't be one-way streets.

Here's a real example of the cost-benefit problem. One time my buddy and I were sitting around jamming some jazz standards together—me on bass, him on a nice Gibson hollow body—and I was like, "Sweet substitutions over the bridge, bro—what have you been praying about lately?"[5]

---

[5] See, when you're a pastor who also happens to be a jazz musician, that's the kind of stream of consciousness, improvisational segue you can drop, and no one will bat an eye.

So he was like, "Lately I've just been praying that God will humble me, you know?"

I dropped a low tone—*bwooowww*, like "bass in ya face means peace see ya later" low—and he stared at me. What? *What?* And I remember shaking my head a little, because that is *not* a prayer you want to pray unless you're deadly serious.

Here's why: God answers prayer.

Despite what it can feel like, God absolutely answers prayers. You think gaining humility is a benefit? Because it'll make you holier or more likable or more like God wants you to be? Sure!

But what's the cost?

See, if you pray to be humbled, God *will* make that happen. But here's the deal: You can't go from proud to humble in a moment. It's not a light switch that can be clicked on and off. The only way to get from proud to humble is by walking a long path. And that path is brutal. The word *humiliating* literally means "humbling."[6] It's a process. And it happens whenever God allows us to experience a situation that is humbling, and then we allow ourselves to be taught and disciplined and transformed by that situation. Then God allows us to repeat that, over and over and over, until a sapling of humility starts to take root in our hard hearts.

My friend who prayed for humility, he was on to something. He was praying for a good thing, and he was praying to a God who loves to answer his kids' prayers. So I'm not making fun of him for asking to be humbled. Honestly. If

---

[6] *Merriam-Webster's Collegiate Dictionary*, 11th ed., s.v. "humiliating."

humility was something he truly wanted, God was going to give it to him, and even though the process might be surprising, my friend would certainly come out the other side as a person closer to the heart of Jesus. Closer to a disciple. There's another churchy word for you: *disciple*. It means a learner or a student, and we are meant to learn from Jesus and be his student as we walk with him through the mess.

RIFFING ON INTIMACY

- How do you respond when God answers one of your prayers with a "no"?
- How can you make prayer more intimate (communication over time)?

3.4

EMBRACE THE CRUTCH

Prayer is essential in this ongoing warfare. Pray hard and long.
EPHESIANS 6:18

Right now, some of you are already at rock bottom. Others are headed that way pretty quickly. You feel like you're out of options. Or you're on top of the world, or headed that way pretty quickly, but wondering when it's all going to come crashing down around you. Because one thing you know for sure is that life is messy.

Wherever you are, the response is the same.

Pray. Pray pray pray.

You've got a whole life of prayer in front of you, and if this is where it all starts—with you crying out to your Creator and Sustainer for help and comfort—then God be praised. Do you think you're the first person to hit rock bottom and come to Jesus? It's been happening since . . . well, since Jesus was walking the shores of the Sea of Galilee and the streets of Jerusalem.

It happened to me, too. After my mom passed, I had exactly two friends who were Christians back at Rutgers. I told one of them about how I was struggling with my mom's death and a bunch of other stuff, and he was like, "Dude, you should pray about that."

And I was like, "Wait, what? How can I *pray* when I don't even know if God is *real*?"

He looked at me like I wasn't the sharpest tool in the shed.

"Just say, 'God, if you're real, I'm open, so reveal yourself to me.'"

Which is how I came to the point of sitting on my bed in my college apartment and saying, "Okay. So . . . I'm probably way out there, but seriously: If you're real—and you probably aren't—I'm here. Reveal yourself to me. I actually do want to know, even though I'm probably just losing my mind."

Want to take a wild guess at what the answer was?

Anyway, sometimes a bit of perspective is helpful, if for no other reason than to help us ignore some of the pundits and the prognosticators who are bursting with hot air. People have been pooh-poohing God, or outright attacking God, since forever, yet God keeps right on answering his children when they cry out to him. The way some people tell it, God is dead. Or they say God is scientifically impossible. Or Western and white. Or mythology. Or a crutch.

But if someone says to you, "Come on, don't you know prayer is a crutch?"—you know what you say back?

"You're right. It is a crutch."

Because the last time I checked, if you break your leg, you're pretty glad to have a crutch! And it isn't *wrong* to lean on a crutch when you have a broken leg.

Or a broken life.

I don't know about you, but I'm messed up. Screwed up and jacked up. Honestly, I'm way past the crutch stage. I need a wheelchair. I need a gurney and an ambulance ride to the hospital. I won't pretend. I can't make it without Jesus. I've tried.

That's where I am. What about you?

Life's messy. So never look down on prayers that rise from the tough times. Just make sure you remember to lift up prayers during the good times too. God hears you, and God wants to be heard. Prayer is a relationship, and the more we pray, the more we build and strengthen that relationship—through *all* of life.

RIFFING ON THE CRUTCH

- How does God want to reveal himself to you and in you?
- How can you better embrace prayer as the crutch for your broken life?

3.5

TRAINING FOR THE RACE

Keep your eyes open. Keep each other's spirits up
so that no one falls behind or drops out.

EPHESIANS 6:18

In real relationships, we *want* to talk all the time, about everything. The dialogue isn't situational, but ongoing. Like when you can't wait to tell your significant other about something awesome or funny that happened to you.

So just like we pray when life is messy, *we need to pray when things are good.*

Here's Paul writing to the Christians in Ephesus again: "Therefore I also, after I heard of your faith in the Lord Jesus and your love for all the saints, do not cease to give thanks for you, making mention of you in my prayers" (Ephesians 1:15-16, NKJV).

When a biblical author uses the word *therefore*, we need to be as attentive as a cat watching a laser pointer. There *will* be something good for us. And here the apostle Paul is like, "Since I've heard about the good stuff you are doing, I'm always praying for you."

When was the last time you did that? Thought of someone who had faith in Jesus, and love for others, and then you prayed a prayer of thanks for that person?

I know—me too. For most of us, crisis precedes prayer. A crisis is often the only reason prayer begins. If everything is smooth sailing, we think we don't need to pray. What would the point be? Now perhaps *think* was too strong a word to use there. Because we mostly don't think about it consciously. We just sort of operate by habit.

You get the kids off to school with lunches and jackets, you get all your errands finished, house cleaned, you have a pleasant family dinner, you play a board game, and you head off to bed. "That was a good day," you sigh to your spouse in bed. You're tired, but the day went well. And you never prayed.

Or you get to the gym, shower, make it to work on time, give a good presentation to your department, lay off the tempting treats in the break room, remember to pick up the dry cleaning on the way home, find a good show on Netflix, and even wash out the popcorn bowl before falling into bed. You're tired, but the day went well. And you never prayed.

Fill in the particulars of your own life here, and the result is often the same. See, it's not like we analyze our days and conclude (read this in your monotone robot voice), "Well, today was sufficiently good, so I didn't need to pray." We aren't that callous. In fact, if we realized we were doing that, we'd probably be disappointed, because most of us agree— at least in theory—that we ought to pray all the time.

Why? It could be fragments of Bible verses from our years in church, like "pray without ceasing" (1 Thessalonians 5:17, NASB). It could be a simple intuition that since some prayer is good, more would be better. Maybe we know that Jesus prayed all the time, or maybe we've observed that the people we look up to spiritually seem to pray more than we do.

Whatever the reason, we know we should, but in practice we usually don't.

Until something bad happens.

Look again, however, at what Paul is telling the Ephesian Christians. He's not praying for them because they're screw-ups. He's not like, "I'm always praying for you because you are a total mangled mess!" (That's what Paul tells the Corinthians, for the record. So it can happen.) It's actually the opposite of that. Basically the people following Jesus in Ephesus were loving God and loving people. Remember how Jesus summed up the entire Old Testament by saying, "Love the Lord your God with all your heart, soul, strength, and mind, and love your neighbor as yourself"? That's what the Ephesians were doing—they were actually fulfilling the greatest commandment! They had it goin' *on*!

And *that* is what makes Paul write to them and say, "Look, you guys are believing in Jesus, you're loving each other, and therefore I don't cease in giving thanks for you, making mention of you in my prayers."

So Paul prays to praise. That's deep! He isn't praying to bash them about problems in this case, but to praise them, and to praise God! And every time he does, he builds up his prayer muscles. In good and bad, big and small, through all the messiness of life, Paul is determined to keep praying.

If we pray only when something bad happens, our prayer muscles aren't prepared. Imagine waking up on a regular

Saturday morning and being like, "Well, I haven't exercised in months, but I'm gonna go run a marathon!" Those twenty-something miles would be torture.[7] But if you train a few times a week, and you do it consistently over time, you'll be ready for that marathon.

Prayer is like a muscle, and the more we use it, the stronger it'll get.

"Lord, my marriage is doing great, thank you! I want to go deeper, I want to be a better spouse."

"God, my finances are not a calamity. Thank you, and help me to be a good steward of the things you've given me."

"Jesus, I'm thinking about Auntie Grace. I'm so glad I know her, and that I get to see her loving you and her family and the folks at the Red Cross where she volunteers. I praise you for her life."

"Father, I like my job. Will you let me be a blessing at work tomorrow, to someone who needs you?"

"Spirit, as I step into this season of my life where I don't have to work every day, will you let me be a good steward of all this time and all this energy, that I may be useful for your Kingdom and your glory?"

"God, I know I'm stuck in traffic right now, but for some reason that colorful tree on the side of the road reminds me: You rock! You're awesome! And thanks for the sweet tunes on the radio!"

If we learn to pray when things are good, then we'll be

---

[7] You can tell running isn't my thing, but I've seen those braggy little stickers on rear windows all around town. Some of those stickers go up into triple digits, which I can only assume means those people have way too much free time, bionic legs, or both.

dialed in when things get bad. We'll have questions, yeah, and pain, but the relationship will be solid. If you're in a relationship like I am, you're constantly relearning the need to remind your loved one how great they are. I truly think my wife is all that and a bag of Cool Ranch Doritos, but sometimes I assume she knows that from me. So instead of saying, "Wow, this is a great meal!" I'm learning to say, "Sweetheart, you are so awesome. Thank you for cooking for me, and thank you for being my companion. You're the love of my life and the person I want to walk through life with."

Once I knew this guy who always flipped directly between extremes. He loved to be contrary. He couldn't help himself. Like if I said I was worried about how many carnitas burritos I was eating, he'd say, "What, so you're never going to eat anything bad for you?" Or if I hit fast-forward on a track, he'd say, "So you hate this band now?"

Don't be that guy. Pray when things are good. Pray when things are normal. Pray when the you-know-what hits the fan. Pray throughout the messiness of life.

All the time, in every circumstance, put your prayer and your praise together.

RIFFING ON TRAINING

- What is going well, right now, that you should be praying about?
- What are some ways you can strengthen your prayer muscles?

3.6

BOWELS? YES, BUT IT'S COMPLICATED

Pray that I'll know what to say and have the courage to say it at the right time, telling the mystery to one and all, the Message that I, jailbird preacher that I am, am responsible for getting out.

EPHESIANS 6:19-20

Now for a few complications. I would love to say God is like a vending machine, and that all we need to do is slip in a few coins of prayer and out pops our desired fancy. But life is messy, Jesus is real, and prayer is *definitely* not simple. So let's get to the nuancing.

And complicating something can be good, right? We're not talking about contradictions. We're talking about adding a few more musicians to the gig. Less simple, more complicated, and hopefully better—and as it relates to prayer, ultimately better for sure. So let's add three instruments to our jam session on prayer.

Here's the first.

When it comes to asking God for something, I have to *really* want something, and want it with the core of who I am. We usually call that core our "heart." Other cultures have located that center of desire in other parts of the body, like the gut. Some Bibles actually translate that word as "bowels"—which is seriously disgusting. But I actually like that, because it reminds me that we're not necessarily talking about "heart issues," like love or romance, but rather about a

97

deep, abiding desire that we feel in the core of who we are. So yeah, I might really want an In-N-Out Burger, especially now that I live north of Portland and the closest Double-Double with Animal Style Fries is a multiple-hour drive away. But do I *really* want that burger? Day after day? Even when I'm not hungry? When I'm praying and washing dishes and playing music and tickling my kids? Do I *still* want it, at the core of who I am?

Now let's add our second instrument.

Let's say I *do* really want something, in my heart and gut. Well then, that thing needs to line up with God. There's a part in John 14, where Jesus is talking to his disciples, and in most versions of the Bible we're used to, he says something like, "Whatever you ask in my name—and remember that I'm united with God the Father—I'll do it" (verses 10-14, author's paraphrase).

So we naturally go, "Really, *whatever*? Sweet . . . I'm gonna ask for a _____."

But "whatever" isn't the key part of that verse. The key actually comes right after that. *In my name.* That needs a bit of teasing out. Does it really mean that attaching the literal name of Jesus to any prayer makes that prayer happen? Like the literal name of Jesus is the special decoder ring to unlock the blessings of God?

I ask for a new car? No car.

I ask for a new car, but in the name of Jesus? *Vroom vroom!* Not really.

So what exactly does "in my name" mean, if not simply

tacking on the name of Jesus to anything we ask for? The biblical idea of "in my name" implies "according to my nature." Like if I say "Daniel Fusco" to the family at Crossroads Community Church, no one thinks of D-A-N-I-E-L space F-U-S-C-O. Instead, they (hopefully) think about their diminutive, hairy, and funny-looking—yet incredibly humble and brilliant—pastor, and they get warm fuzzies inside. It's not about the letters of my name—it's about *me*!

I like the way one contemporary version of the Bible puts it. Listen to this: "whatever you request *along the lines of who I am and what I am doing*, I'll do it" (John 14:13). I added the italics, because I love how that captures what's really going on here. If we're going after the same things Jesus is going after, then *of course* God is going to answer that prayer in the affirmative! Because *not* granting that would mean working *against* God's own purposes!

If you ask for a lifetime supply of donuts, why in the world would God grant that? It only builds your waistline and cholesterol, not God's blessed Kingdom. But if you ask for, say, a better ability to love people? God's going to be all over that!

Which brings us to our third instrument.

Let's say that first, you really want something, at the "bowels" of your being. And let's say that second, what you want lines up with what God wants and God is doing. Like instead of wanting a hamburger, you want humility. What then?

Well, then God *does* it. God gives you what you ask. The jam session of prayer is in full harmony. You're walking through life in rhythm with God's music.

Now, remember what I said about complications? Even with all those instruments in harmony, there's another piece to all of this that we don't really like to talk about.

Sometimes we ask God for something, and God answers and gives it to us, *but it takes a lifetime for it to arrive.*

Sometimes when we pray, we're asking for faith—or joy or peace or patience—without the life circumstances that will force us to grow in that. We want more love, but only so we can love people who are already lovable. We want more self-control, but only when it comes to habits and behaviors we can already control.

So another way of looking at the cost-benefit issue, in biblical terms, is to say we want the fruit without the growth. But growth doesn't work like that.

The Psalms, which are a collection of prayers and songs written to God, cover every human emotion: wonder, despair, contentment, jealousy, you name it. It's why people love the Psalms so much. They are honest and raw. Real humanity is on display. And in the very first psalm, the poet shares something important about growth and fruit.

> Blessed is the one
> > who does not walk in step with the wicked
> or stand in the way that sinners take
> > or sit in the company of mockers,
> but whose delight is in the law of the LORD,
> > and who meditates on his law day and night.

That person is like a tree planted by streams of water,
    which yields its fruit in season
and whose leaf does not wither—
    whatever they do prospers.

PSALM 1:1-3, NIV

In the word picture the poet is using, the clean water that a tree needs to grow is compared to delighting in God's teaching—and not just delighting *in*, but meditating *on*. To *meditate* means, basically, to chew on it and get all the flavor and nourishment out of it. Day after day, week after week, year after year. We know what happens when a tree is allowed to grow in such conditions: It thrives!

That's exactly how it unfolds in Psalm 1: The tree bears fruit, at God's appointed time, and it remains healthy and growing. It prospers.

And *you* can be that tree!

Isn't that what we want? To be fruitful? To grow and prosper? Aren't those the people we admire and aspire to be like? But we *must* remain planted. Season after season. Because we're all in process, and there is no shortcut to growth.

RIFFING ON COMPLICATIONS
- How can you better pray from your "bowels,"
  in accordance with what God wants and is doing?
- What fears might be holding you back from
  joining God?

3.7

WALK BY FAITH

*When we trust in him, we're free to say whatever needs
to be said, bold to go wherever we need to go.*

EPHESIANS 3:12

Life is messy, but life is also—for most of us—pretty long. Being a tree that bears fruit can feel like it takes freakin' *forever*. Which is why, understandably, along the way we tend to pray for things we need or want.

But the elephant in the room remains: Why doesn't God give us what we ask for when we ask for something good, and something he could take care of right away?

In some ways, it's almost easier to make sense of the huge prayers that go unanswered than it is to make sense of the smaller ones that go unanswered.

If God is God—and yes, I do believe that!—then there are plans and purposes that God has for our lives. One of the ways God helps us to take the next step is by sometimes saying no to our prayers, even when they seem like good prayers.

Like, why didn't God heal so-and-so's cancer? That's a tough one, as I know from personal experience. But sometimes God says no to a good prayer because there is something even better in store. Like in the NFL draft, when a player gets picked in one of the later rounds. That's tough to swallow for that player, who feels like he deserved to be chosen higher. But sometimes, a year or two later, that player is overjoyed to be lifting up the Lombardi trophy!

So God's initial no can set off a series of events that are even better than we imagined. We simply can't know, this side of heaven, what higher purposes were served by so-and-so not being healed—but if that person is already in heaven, you can be sure they're rejoicing in God's no, because now they can see the entire picture, even when we cannot. Even when it's still brutal for us, here in the mess.

But even if we can deal with the big stuff, it's the smaller unanswered prayers that can challenge our daily faith. The stuff that seems like it would be *so easy* for God to take care of.

Like when you ask to get the job offer. Or when you want to be the one picked to rent the apartment. Or when someone just needs a small blessing or encouragement. Prayers like that aren't asking God to move the earth!

And yet there are times when God says no to these as well. It's messy. And I wish prayer made sense more of the time! It's often said that when God does something that we don't understand, we need to rely on what we *do* understand about God.

Isaiah 55, and most of Job, and many of the Psalms, and pretty much every time Jesus talks to his disciples—all of that reminds me of two truths.

That I can't always understand God.

And that God knows I can't always understand.

Sometimes—and I apologize for sounding like a bumper sticker again, but again it's true!—sometimes we have to walk by faith. And do you know what the huge problem is when it comes to walking by faith?

That we have to walk by faith!

RIFFING ON FAITH

- Has God ever answered your prayer in an entirely unexpected way and/or with entirely unexpected timing?
- Where in your life is it currently challenging to walk by faith?

3.8

IMITATE GOD

Watch what God does, and then you do it, like children
who learn proper behavior from their parents.

EPHESIANS 5:1

Walking by faith requires us to know what God *wants*, right? We can't walk down a path if we don't know where the path is. We can't *do* a thing until we know what that thing *is*.

Which is logical, and sounds true—but which creates a subtle trap that can stop us from walking at all!

The thinking goes like this:

I should do what God wants me to do.

Wait—what does God want me to do, exactly?

I should find out.

And I shouldn't do anything else until *I find out.*

After all, I don't want to do the wrong thing!

Then weeks or years or decades later, we discover that we were so busy trying to "figure out what God wanted" that we walked precisely nowhere! Knowledge can be a good thing, but it can also paralyze. Many of us suffer from this type of analysis paralysis.

Which is exactly why the Bible recommends another technique: imitation.

Imitate God, just like a much-loved child imitates his parents. That's what Ephesians 5:1 tells us, and it's genius, because we can start to imitate *without* complete knowledge. When we're imitating, we don't have to know up front everything God wants us to do. Instead, we can look at God and what God is doing, and then take one step. One step leads to another, and another after that. It's exactly how small children learn virtually everything—by imitating their parents and siblings one step at a time.

As we walk through the mess, God isn't calling us to be people who *talk* about God.

Wait, let me rephrase that: God isn't calling us to be people who *only* talk about God, but to be people who talk *and* walk. Jesus isn't asking his followers to pass a test about what God wants and *then* start living. Rather, we should learn how God acts, and then say, "I want to be like God."

And how do we learn how God acts? Finally, a simple question! We've already talked about developing communication and intimacy with him through prayer, and that's part of it. The other part? We look at Jesus.

While he was on earth, Jesus told his friends that anyone who had seen *him* had seen God the Father. The Bible tells us that Jesus is the exact representation of God. As many have put it in a memorable way over the years, "Jesus is God with skin on." And as one of my main men, Thomas Merton, puts it, "Jesus is the theology of the Father."[8]

So if Jesus did something on earth, it's a good bet that we're meant to imitate him. Don't fall into the trap of thinking you need to know everything about God or what God wants before you start walking. We can open up the Bible, read one page of one of the Gospels, and have *plenty* to "walk" for the next week! It's all about becoming children and imitating our Father. Imitating Jesus. That's what the walk is. That's what life is.

Consider work. You've probably heard that hiring family members can lead to trouble. Well, one of the most depressing things I hear as a pastor, over and over, is Christian business leaders telling me, "Yeah, I try to never hire Christians."

I used to ask why, but I don't bother anymore, because the reason is always the same. Too often, Christian workers hired by a Christian boss take advantage of the fact that they are brothers and sisters in God's family. Because if they show up late, or slack off, or turn in a poorly researched report, what's the big deal, since none of that matters as much as the fact that Jesus died for our sins?

---

[8] Thomas Merton, *No Man Is an Island* (New York: Harvest, 1983), 23.

Except it *is* a big deal, because doing a terrible job at work means we aren't walking the walk—we aren't imitating God!

When people take advantage of the gospel to be lazy, that destroys the witness of the people of God. If an agnostic coworker, or a coworker of another faith (including atheists, since atheism absolutely requires as much faith as any religion) sees you slacking, what does that person learn about God from you?

In fact, being brothers and sisters in the Lord should actually have the *opposite* effect: It should make us work *harder* for each other. We should say, "Hey, we're *family*, and that counts for a lot. I'm not going to take advantage of you or goof off. I'm going to be a blessing by serving hard and well!" Because that's what families do. That's what Jesus did.

If you orient your heart and your mind and your soul toward God, trying to imitate him, your fellow workers will be blessed.

Notice that what we're talking about makes the shape of the cross. In the case of our jobs, we work vertically. We're serving Jesus. We're doing it for Jesus, and it doesn't matter if anyone else is watching us. You know that cheesy refrigerator magnet people have—"*Dance like no one's watching*"? It's true with work: What we do shouldn't change if our boss is watching or not, because it's not about our boss. It's about honoring our Creator, who created us to work. One of the first blessings God gives to humans—ever, way back in the Garden of Eden—is the blessing of *work*. Work is part of God's perfect creation, even before we start sinning things up!

Do you want to walk at work the way God wants you to walk? You can start tomorrow! Don't work for a paycheck. Don't work for your boss. Work for God, just like Jesus did. Your boss will be blessed, you'll be honoring God, *and* you'll get your paycheck.

Things aren't any different with parenting: imitate God, imitate Jesus.

Recently I heard someone refer to parents raising their kids Christian as "brainwashing."

Think about that for a second or two.

I know, right? Talk about a blind spot! So let's say I *don't* raise my kids Christian, and instead raise them a different religion. Or agnostic. Or atheistic. Yep, that's brainwashing them just as much as if I raise them Christian! *Brainwashing is simply a shortcut for education that someone doesn't like.* Anti-war? The US military is brainwashing our youth. Anti-consumerism? TV commercials are brainwashing us. Our kids' brains are gonna get washed with *something*, I guarantee you, and I'd like to make sure they're getting washed by Jesus, rather than by anything else!

So if you're a parent, imitate God. The Bible tells us that every family on earth takes its shape from God, and that's one reason why the Bible is full of the language of the family. Mind-blowing! Ask yourself how God treats his kids. What did Jesus do when he encountered children? Start walking, start imitating, and you'll find that you didn't need all the answers up front because God showed you what you needed along the journey. Proverbs 4:18 says that the path of the righteous is "like the first gleam of dawn, which shines ever brighter until the full light of day" (NLT). Isn't that a relief? We can start while the path is still dusky, walking in the trust that God will continue to reveal what is needed to make it through the mess.

Church works the same way. If you've been around Christians for any amount of time, you will have heard discussion about how to get people to church.

That's the wrong discussion.

Imitating God isn't about getting people to walk through the front doors of our churches—it's about our churches walking out into the world where the people are! Because that's exactly what God did for us when he sent Jesus to earth. The church is meant to go out into the world! Into all neighborhoods and nations! It's not enough to put up service times on the signboard. We've got to go out, hang out, get to know folks, and then invite them to be a part of the family of faith. Just as God treats us—the church, God's kids—we are to treat our community and our world. God didn't stay in a holy huddle in heaven, but became one of us. Talk about walking *through* the mess!

God wants us to be like him, to imitate him. That means becoming fully identified with our community, yet not *partaking* in the things our community does that are in rebellion against God. When we walk into the world to God's rhythm and heartbeat, we're marching to a different drummer, and that's attractive.

In short, if we want to walk like Jesus, we associate, not

participate. You've heard the saying "hate the sin and love the sinner"? That's solid!

Think about the alternatives. Love the sin and love the sinner? Pretty sure God does *not* want us to love sin! Hate the sin *and* hate the sinner? That's a terrible idea, and it's the opposite of how God treats us.[9] Romans 5:8 tells us that "God demonstrates his own love for us in this: *While we were still sinners*, Christ died for us" (NIV). Thank God!

Jesus was fully God and fully human, which meant that he *associated* with us, but didn't *participate* in our sin. That's the sweet spot. That's the mess in the middle. Association without full participation. Jesus loved us with a love so deep that he willingly died in our place—while we were *still* sinners, remember!—yet he never sinned. That makes him the textbook example of "hate the sin and love the sinner."

And let me reassure you, so there isn't any doubt: you are *not* your sin. You are God's beloved child. God hates your sin, because sin by its very definition is hateful, *but God does not hate you*. If you've been taught that God hates you, memorize Romans 5:8 as an antidote, along with John 3:16-17 (NIV)— "For God so loved the world that he gave his one and only Son, that whoever believes in him shall not perish but have eternal life. For God did not send his Son into the world to condemn the world, but to save the world through him"— and 1 Timothy 2:4 (NIV)—"[God] wants all people to be saved and to come to a knowledge of the truth." God loves

---

9 Not that this has stopped certain churches and individuals from trying the "hate the sinner" approach. I won't dignify them by mentioning their names, but let's just say that they aren't bringing too many folks into the Kingdom, nor representing God's heart well!

you, but God doesn't love everything that you do. God loves us even with full disclosure that we do things that God hates. Like we said earlier, God loves us because God is love, not because we are perfectly lovable. Now that rocks!

Your friends and neighbors and coworkers know life is messy, but they probably don't believe the church has any answers. Man, I never wanted to go to church as a kid—and now that I'm a pastor, I *have* to go! And I love it! God's funny like that. But seriously, are you going to wait for their opinion about church to magically change and for them to flood in on Sunday morning, or are you going to take this good news to *them*?

Which did Jesus do for us?

Imitate God, just as a much-loved child imitates his parents.

That's it. That's the way God asks his kids to walk, plain and simple. At work, at home, at church—everywhere we are, whatever we're doing, we're invited to ask ourselves what Jesus would do. Then, because he's a father full of love, God cheers us on as we walk.

RIFFING ON IMITATION

- In what ways do you want to start imitating God?
- How can you, like Jesus, bring God out into the open?

CODA

I love how the Bible gives followers of Jesus marching orders, almost literally, in Ephesians 4:1-2:

I want you to get out there and walk—better yet, run!—on the road God called you to travel. I don't want any of you sitting around on your hands. I don't want anyone strolling off, down some path that goes nowhere.

Jesus chose to become one of us. Then he went where he needed to go and said what he needed to say. Like we saw, he kept the end in mind.

For him that looked like prayer. Bravery. Endurance. Doing the little things. Lots more prayer. Doing the big things.

So how would *your* life look if you decided to walk the way Jesus walked?

Honestly, there are only two right answers to that.

It would be unpredictable, and it would be good.

See, the Spirit is infinitely creative! You don't sign up to follow Jesus because you know what'll happen and you want to get on board. You sign up because you have absolutely no idea *what* will happen but you can't wait to find out. You take the leap of faith. You know that Jesus may not be safe, but he's good.[10]

But you'd also be free to flourish. To live a life of surprising and overwhelming joy. That's *shalom*, and it's how our lives are meant to go down.

When I think about trying to walk like that though? Dang. It's hard. *So* hard.

---

[10] Borrowed from a description of Aslan the lion: "'Safe?' said Mr. Beaver. . . . 'Who said anything about safe? 'Course he isn't safe. But he's good. He's the King, I tell you.'" C. S. Lewis, *The Lion, the Witch and the Wardrobe* (New York: HarperCollins), 81.

But on those times I do it? So *good*.

That's our job. As Ephesians 4:4-6 puts it, "You were all called to travel on the same road and in the same direction, so stay together, both outwardly and inwardly. You have one Master, one faith, one baptism, one God and Father of all, who rules over all, works through all, and is present in all."

Check out how that job description—the way we're supposed to walk—ends: "Everything you are and think and do is permeated with Oneness" (Ephesians 4:6).

There's mystery here, for sure, but it's the good kind of mystery!

Still, we know that God is *calling* us to walk on a road that he's *prepared and equipped us to walk on*.

And as we walk, God wants us to keep one thing in mind above all others. That quality is what our final section is all about. And it truly needs no introduction. Because love never fails.

PART IV

PSALM

THE BEGINNING OF THE END

*Long before he laid down earth's foundations, he had us in mind, had
settled on us as the focus of his love, to be made whole and holy by his love.*

EPHESIANS 1:4

Immense in mercy and with an incredible love, he embraced us.

EPHESIANS 2:4

*Mostly what God does is love you. Keep company
with him and learn a life of love.*

EPHESIANS 5:1-2

Well, here you are, entering the last section of the book.

Did you read straight through? Are you starting here?
Have you been skipping around, trying to find something—
anything—that will speak your language? And you saw the
title of this section and thought, "Now *that's* for me!"

No matter how you got here, welcome!

To be honest with you, I can't imagine writing a book
with this much Jesus in it and *not* ending with a section on
love. Even in the midst of our messy lives and the unpredict-
ability and things we don't understand, Jesus is all about love.
Jesus loves us in and through it all, to the end, just like his
disciples (John 13:1). We can talk all we want about the mess
and the good news and how to walk through all of it, but *we
need to keep love over and under and through all of it.*

Love is the centerpiece of Jesus' message. Love was how he
thought and operated. He rocked his disciples' worlds by telling

117

them to love even their *enemies*. When Jesus was asked about the greatest two commandments, he picked ones all about love. And the fruit of the Holy Spirit is love too! Between faith, hope, and love—all great—Paul says that love is the greatest (see 1 Corinthians 13:13). And in Ephesians 5:1 Paul exhorts the church in Ephesus to "walk in love."

Love is everywhere in our Bibles, because as 1 John 4:8 puts it, "God is love" (NIV). God is the God of the mess. And God is love.

But here's the thing about love: *It can't be understood simply by defining it!* Defining love can be part of it, but true love is something that is experienced. When you love, when you are loved, you *know* it. You can't exactly explain it, but you also can't help *trying* to explain it.

I can't help it either!

So for this last section, I want you to read the same way you'd watch the sky during a Fourth of July fireworks display. Every summer as a kid in central New Jersey, I watched with awe as the sky filled with falling fire.[1] And at the climax of any fireworks show, the reaction is always the same.

Ooh! Aah!

It's pure colorful mayhem, with the fireworks exploding at such a rapid pace, with such precision and power, that it reminds me of the culmination of John Coltrane's *A Love Supreme*.

This final section is going to be like the end of an epic fireworks display.

---

[1] Now that I live in southern Washington, where fireworks are legal, I watch with awe as everyone and their mom sets off whatever they want, wherever and whenever they want to!

I'm going to share with you some more stories about some of my favorite things: baseball, food, and my big fat Italian family. Why? Because I want us to be able to see love over and under and through the mess. I want "love in action" to explode across the sky of our imaginations.

Because love is what unites everything we've been talking about. The messiness of life. How we're worse off than we think and how the good news is better than we can imagine. How Jesus calls us to walk it out, beside him. Love unites *all* of that.

So I want us, during the final part of our riff on Ephesians, to focus our hearts and minds on God's great love for us, and on our love for others. I want us to *ooh!* and *aah!* in wonder and appreciation. I want us to start understanding—at a heart-level—that the love of God permeates this messy life. That God's love is the foundation of our grace-and-peace remedy.

RIFFING ON LOVE

- How does God's love fit into the idea of a messy life?
- How do you see God's love reflected into your life presently?

4.2

A MESS OF LOVE AND LIFE

Observe how Christ loved us. His love was not cautious but extravagant. He didn't love in order to get something from us but to give everything of himself to us. Love like that.

EPHESIANS 5:1-2

I come by my sports obsession honestly. My grandfather was a longtime football coach, and my father always loved baseball. My dad grew up near Ebbets Field, where the famed Brooklyn Dodgers played—and his playing stickball with the son of legendary Dodger Gil Hodges didn't hurt, either. When I was growing up, my dad was always my Little League coach, and we'd watch ball games together on TV whenever we could. That's where I learned how to yell at the television. But I digress.

It seemed like all my friends played baseball too. We always got split up onto different Little League teams, which meant that most weekends I was playing against one of my buddies. We all played together on the high school team, but in Little League we played against each other. All baseball, all the time.

One Little League game, my good friend John was on the opposing team. We'd spent the school day talking smack, and by the time the ump yelled "Play ball!" we were all jacked up to win. Our teams were vying for first place, but we would have played to win against each other no matter what. *Honor* was on the line. Not to mention bragging rights.

In the first inning, I'm catching, and John lands on second base with a stand-up double. He starts chirping at me from the bag. "I can't wait for the collision at the plate, Fusco! This is gonna be fun!"

I can't say much with my mask on, plus I'm concentrating on staying in front of each pitch, but John won't let up. Chirp chirp chirp.

And sure enough, the next batter goes deep into the count

and then smacks a single into shallow right. John's going all the way, no matter what his third-base coach tells him. He knows it. I know it. I toss my mask behind me, stand out in front of the plate, and bring up my glove for the throw from right field. But I'm also keeping one eye on John, and he takes like the widest turn ever around third and is absolutely barreling down on me. He's a big guy, all square edges and Italian confidence, and I'm pretty small still, even with all my gear on.

Everything unfolds in slow motion. I see the vein popping in his neck and hear his husky breath. I'm his prey, a sitting duck. The throw is in the air, and I just need to catch the ball and hang on to it. It's gonna hurt, but it doesn't matter. So here comes the ball, and here comes John, and I catch the ball a split second before he's on me. And it isn't pretty—I get laid *out*. Like forearm-to-the-chin, slide-until-I-hit-the-backstop laid out.

I watch the ball rolling slowing across the dirt and hear the ump yell "Safe!" just as John steps over me, a gigantic smirk on his face. He's just rung my bell, and we both know it. He totally has bragging rights now. Rats!

Dad is laughing and shaking his head from the dugout. "Nice play, John!"

And Grandpa is on my case from the stands. "Danny, come on. You got to hold on to that ball!"

As John walks back to his dugout and I try to patch up my shredded dignity, the ump warns both benches, "No more contact at the plate. This is Little League, for cryin' out loud, not the bigs!"

Next inning, it's my turn to hit. Digging in, I don't say a word to John, who's catching. And he's still chirping, enjoying his moment of victory. And I can't say anything. Rats! I just sit tight, trying to put the past inning behind me. I make the pitcher work for it by slapping a few balls foul, and before long I'm trotting to first with a walk. I steal second on the next pitch, which gets away from John, and still I don't say anything to him. I take a lead, and sure enough, the batter laces a single into right.

Oh yeah, baby! It's *on*. Payback time. I take the same not-slowing-down turn at third, ignoring my base coach's shouts, and pretty soon I've got John in my crosshairs. Dirt's flying off my cleats, I'm tensing every muscle in my body, and I'm picturing myself as a train. Here comes the throw from right, here comes the Fusco train, and *bam!*—John's on his back, I'm leaping to my feet, and the ball's dribbling across the dirt. Safe!

And more important, revenge! I sense the baseball gods applauding my fearlessness! My dad and my grandfather are beaming with pride. I'm just chugging the adrenaline and feeling pubescently powerful.

Then the ump shouts, "Fusco, you are *gone*. Out of the game for contact at the plate!"

Who cares? I'm on top of the world.

Dad's not, though. He's livid. "Now come on, Harold!" he's yelling. "These guys play ball in high school. They're friends! John laid Dan out, so Dan *had* to do that! You know that! And this is a big game! *Come on!*"

But the ump just keeps shaking his head, having none of it. "I warned 'em, Tom. He's outta here!"

Dad goes ballistic. Like old-school-Brooklyn ballistic. Like eternity and justice hang in the balance. With his Italian New York accent more pronounced than ever, he rails on the ump. "This is un-freakin-believable! They're playing for a shot at the championship, and you toss one of our best players? Don't be a jerk, Harold! Now let . . ."

The ump cuts him off. "Now *you're* outta here, Tom!" and he slams his mask into the dirt for emphasis.

I like that Dad's sticking up for me, but now there are *two* Fuscos down and out. Seems like the ump's forgotten we brought along *three*, though, because he turns his back on Grandpa. I have to admire Grandpa. Usually he's so mild mannered, which is what makes his tantrum so epic. He starts screaming, he's tossing cups, he's shaking the chain-link fence, he's suggesting things about how the umpire feels about his mother and his sister. And before too long, both teams and all the fans are watching in shocked silence as three generations of Fuscos trudge toward our Lincoln Town Car, Grandpa still yelling every step of the way. It's Little League folklore of epic proportions—even *Grandpa* getting thrown off the complex!

I bet you can picture that, right? That's Jersey style right there, for sure!

And here's the reason I told that story: It's a taste of Love Supreme.

See, the minute we hit the car and Grandpa stopped ranting, the three of us started laughing, and we couldn't stop.

We ended up going out for ice cream together, and reenacting the incident. I should have been playing for first place still, but instead I was watching my grandpa wave around his ice cream cone, watching my dad give his best impression of the angry umpire. Even the bruises I'd acquired from John slamming into me—and me slamming into him!—felt good. Not just badges of honor, but signs that I'd done what needed doing. As a player and as a man. I'd chased after something, with my family cheering me on.

Fast-forward to today, with Grandpa in his nineties, Dad in his seventies, and me in my forties, and we *still* belly laugh about that day. We've talked about it at dozens of meals over the years, and as many times as we've started to giggle—"Remember when . . ."—that's the same number of times Grandma has shaken her head and tut-tutted.

It was a mess! Three generations of one family getting tossed from a Little League game is a mess!

So much love displayed in the midst of my crazy family. All the noise, the chaos, the relationships . . . about a child's baseball game—and yet about something so much bigger. My family got kicked out of the game *because we were so full of love that day*. Those family memories, those treasured relationships, they're one of God's favorite ways of giving his kids a taste of Love Supreme.

. . .

Know what else is a taste of love? *My grandma's cooking.*

My *seriously* large extended family hits almost every single

Italian/Jersey stereotype. Like, whatever stereotype you're picturing right now? True—but even more exaggerated!

So *of course* my grandmother and my mother were amazing cooks. Still are! And in my family, food was a love language. They fed those that they loved. Before I could ride a bike I was digging into spaghetti with garlic and oil or chowing down on shrimp scampi over fettuccini. A single bite of anything Grandma made was a life-altering experience.

So naturally, when I went to college, I did what most freshman guys do: turned vegetarian.

It wasn't for the animals' sake, either—it was for mine. During my first week, I stared through the cafeteria sneeze-guard at a parade of meats that just looked . . . *wrong*. And they tasted worse. I didn't know much, but I knew meatloaf wasn't supposed to be gray, and chicken wasn't supposed to feel like rubber when I tried to chew it. So I called it quits as a carnivore and reluctantly converted to a salad-and-cereal diet.

At least until my first visit home. Back in my grandmother's kitchen while she cooked, I breathed in deep through my nose. Rosemary, stewed tomatoes, garlic, and the sweet savor of sausage and peppers. It was good to be back in the land of real food—so good that I wanted to hang on to it.

"Grandma," I said around a mouthful of stolen bread that I had conveniently dropped in the saucepan, "you gotta teach me how to cook some of this stuff—the food's *so bad* at college. Look, I've already lost *fifteen* pounds!"

I patted my stomach for dramatic effect.

She glanced up from the pot she was stirring, *tsk-tsk*'ed at how her grandson was wasting away before her eyes, and began to narrate her cooking for me. The next minutes were filled with "just a pinch of this, or more if you feel like more," "just long enough to bring out the spice," and "your grandfather would eat this for breakfast if I let him!" Nothing was written, and everything was guided by her nose, her taste buds, and her decades of experience. The look on her face told me she was *loving* it.

At first I felt confident. Like, *I could totally make that!* I began to picture the romantic possibilities at college if I could cook up a storm. Hel-*lo*, ladies!

But as my grandmother's instructions piled up and blurred together, I began to realize that it would take a lot longer than half an hour to learn a lifetime of cooking wisdom. "Grandma," I finally burst out, "you never use recipes, so how come everything still tastes so *good*?"

She smiled from ear to ear, and probably would have reached up to pinch my cheek if her hands hadn't been buried in a bowl of salad ingredients. "Danny," she cooed—and sorry to interrupt the quote, but here you should *definitely* read with an exaggerated New York Italian accent—"my cooking tastes so good because I put a lot of love into it!"

Now that I'm so much older and wiser than I was in college (ahem), I know that with practice, anyone can cook a decent chicken parmigiana. But to cook chicken parmigiana that makes all others taste like warm cardboard? That takes some serious love. Love was the secret ingredient that

Grandma added to absolutely everything she cooked. And she was right: That was why her food tasted *so* good.

Now, since this is a book more about Jesus than my grandma, let's connect her cooking to Jesus.[2]

One of Jesus' disciples and friends, John, writes about this in 1 John 4, but I'm going to paraphrase and shorten it a bit:

> Friends, let's love each other!
>
> Since love comes from God, we can know God
> by truly loving each other—just like a lack of love is
> a sign that we don't know God.
>
> And we know God loves us like this: God sent his
> Son, Jesus, to live with us and to love us, so that we
> could learn how to live and love in the same way.
>
> That's one reason we ought to love each other . . .
> we might not be able to see God, but we can't miss
> the evidence of God's love all around us when we
> love each other.

Isn't that a rad riff on love? My Italian grandmother *cooks* the way God does *everything.*

With unbelievable love.

And here's the crazy part. She doesn't cook with love *after* I tell her how much I enjoy her food—she cooks with love *before* anyone sits down to eat. Her love is preemptive, so it sweetens everything she prepares, no matter who is sitting down to eat it.

---

[2] And by the way, I know pastors aren't supposed to put words in Jesus' mouth, but if he ever tasted my grandma's food, he would be like, "Sister, every day I need to eat at your house!" And Grandma would have fed Jesus plump, to the glory of God!

That's *exactly* how it is with God. God loves us *before* we come to him. The Bible is chock-full of stories designed to tell us exactly that. Think of King David, the author of a ton of the Psalms, who wrote a praise song (Psalm 139) about how God knew him and loved him while he was still in his mother's womb. Or think back to chapter 2.2, where we saw how Jesus, along with God the Father and God the Spirit, set in motion the rescue plan for humanity before you or I even existed.

See what's going on?

Love comes from God. When we love each other, we're showing each other that we've had a taste of what God is like. And when we love each other *preemptively*, we're giving the world—strangers, neighbors, enemies, and absolutely everybody—a picture of God.

Here's what we're chasing. *Love is meant to be experienced.* Love Supreme is not just an idea or a concept. It's real, it's lived, it stirs our emotions. It makes us lose our minds sometimes for those we love, because our hearts are so full.

Look, it doesn't matter *who* is coming over for dinner. Family, friends, strangers . . . even enemies. What matters is that we cook with love, ahead of time, just in case, because that's the way to taste a Love Supreme.

RIFFING ON EXTRAVAGANCE

- When have you seen extravagant love lived out?
- How do you feel, knowing that God loved you before you even existed?

4.3

THE REAL SHAPE OF LOVE

*God wants us to grow up, to know the whole truth and tell it in
love—like Christ in everything. We take our lead from Christ,
who is the source of everything we do. He keeps us in step with
each other. His very breath and blood flow through us, nourishing
us so that we will grow up healthy in God, robust in love.*

EPHESIANS 4:15-16

I hope you dug those concrete examples of love. Every family
has its own stories like that, of times when love is over and
under and through the mess.

But now we need to hear something. Are you ready? I
hope so, because I'm just dying to tell you. The good news
we need to hear again. And again. And again.

Do you want the gospel?

I do. I want it and need it. Every minute of every day. We
all need the gospel as much today as when we first heard and
responded:

Walk in love, as Christ loved us and gave himself up
for us.

EPHESIANS 5:2, ESV

Soak that up.

It's everything. Not just love supreme, but *Love Supreme.*

At least for me, that love is everything. I won't speak for
you, but I don't deserve it. Not one bit. I haven't earned it and

I'm not entitled to it. I didn't do anything to help my case. In fact, I *hurt* my case, constantly, and like I said before—and I'll say it until I die—God loves me anyway, not because I'm lovable, but because God is love. God *so* loved me that he came up with a plan to rescue me, even though it would cost him dearly. Me! I'm that guy who doesn't deserve love in the first place!

Then once God had given me that reference point for what true love looks like, he gave me my marching orders. Or *walking* orders, I should say.

"Walk in love, as Christ loved us and gave himself up for us."

That's heavy, isn't it? That God wants us to love people—to walk in love—in the same way Jesus loves us.

In other words, loving people irrespective of our feelings for them. Regardless of whether they deserve our love, or anyone's love. Did you ever hear of the Law of Reciprocal Affection? (Probably not—who talks like that besides professors?) Let me explain it to you. It says that if you love me and give me what I want, then I'll love you and give you what you want. It reminds me of the infamous Soup Nazi from *Seinfeld*, who was happy to give his customers what they wanted, as long as they knew their order by the time they reached the front of the line. Otherwise, "No soup for you!"[3]

Isn't that how we often function? How everything around us functions? Scratch my back and I'll scratch yours—but cut *me* off and I'll cut *you* off.

[3] "The Best of the Soup Nazi," YouTube, July 13, 2008, https://www.youtube.com/watch?v=M2lfZg-apSA.

God, on the other hand . . . I mean, no human could have invented a deity who functions like God does, not in a million years! When I push God away, God draws me *closer*. That's like the Law of One-Way Affection, where God keeps loving us even when we're hating him!

Remember the story of the Prodigal Son, who takes his dad's cash and blows every cent on women and wine, only to come crawling back home, hoping to fend off starvation by begging for a minimum-wage job with his dad's business? In that story, the dad is God, and watch what God does to his rebellious, ungrateful, good-for-nothing kid:

> While he was still a long way off, his father saw him coming. Filled with love and compassion, he ran to his son, embraced him, and kissed him.
>
> LUKE 15:20, NLT

The father's response in that parable makes zero sense. Zero! Unless God is who God says he is.

Walking in love, God's way . . . that's beyond heavy. It's impossible—unless we receive God's power, through the help of God's Spirit, based on what Jesus did.

See, we're *so* messed up, it's like it takes an entire *team*—almost like the Trinity, if I can make the comparison—to save us!

"Walk in love, as Christ loved us and gave himself up for us."

On our own, we can't love like that.

I can't do it. You can't do it. I mean, you've tried, right? God knows I have. And the result is always the same.

Failure.

But God can do it, in us and through us. God's love, God's power, they need to be in the driver's seat. That's why I love to pray like this: "*Please*, teach me how to love that person, because on my own, I'm not going to get it right—and you know that better than anyone, Lord. I want to love. Will you teach me how to love?"

I know without a doubt that there is only one thing in this universe that can overcome the enormity of my failure, and that is the enormity of God's love.

RIFFING ON THE SHAPE OF LOVE

- Where in your life do you need God to teach you how to love?
- Which specific relationships need God's preemptive and proactive love?

4.4

LOVE, NEGATIVELY

I don't want any of you sitting around on your hands. I don't want anyone strolling off, down some path that goes nowhere. And mark that you do this with humility and discipline—not in fits and starts, but steadily, pouring yourselves out for each other in acts of love, alert at noticing differences and quick at mending fences.

EPHESIANS 4:2-3

Here's the thing: That "walking in love" stuff sounds great, but we need to be honest about it. The messiness of life involves real people and real problems and real pain. None of that is solved merely by a *God Is Love* bumper sticker or stories about cooking and baseball.

Part of the answer is the positive reality that God *is* love . . . but part of that truth includes negatives. See, godly love in action *must* include things you *can't* do.

Look, the Bible gets a lot of grief—and, by extension, so does God—because of the negatives. God is a cosmic killjoy, and the Bible becomes a giant list of seemingly awesome stuff we can't do.

Two things. First, the Bible does have some pretty impressive lists of negatives in it. But second, they're in the Bible for a good reason! God loves us too much to allow us to hurt ourselves.

Third—and this is a bonus point for you just because I'm feeling extra generous—I'm going to suggest that you *want* the negatives when it comes to love, even if you don't think you do. If our discussion back on pages 71–72 about how Jesus is going to *annihilate* evil didn't convince you of that, I hope the next few paragraphs do.

When the Bible gives a list of negatives, it usually involves a warning not to "deceive" ourselves. Basically what it's saying is, "Don't trick yourself into thinking that the 'good' stuff you do gives you license to be evil at the same time." God loves us enough to not want us to remain ignorant. Last time I checked, most people don't take too kindly to ignorance, right? We use that term to insult people, not praise them.

So James 3 asks the rhetorical questions: Can salt water and fresh water come from the same spring (verse 11)? And can the same tongue both bless God and celebrate evil (verse 10)? Or help someone and tear someone down? Same deal in the "love chapter," 1 Corinthians 13, where we're told what love *is*—like patient, kind, and full of hope—and also what love is *not*—like not envious, not boastful, and not keeping records of wrongs.

So those lists of "do nots" that pop up in the Bible are *essential* to defining God's love.

Want to get to the top of the mountain? Take *this* path, but *not* that path.

Want to fix that annoying screech in your car's engine? Use *this* part, but *not* that part.

Just as walking in love *requires* specific actions, so walking in love must also *prohibit* specific other actions. It can't be, "Yeah, I love you and I'm going to smile at you and then stab you in the back." That isn't love. That can't be love.

Walking God's way is the fruit of the Spirit: love, joy, peace, patience, kindness, goodness, faithfulness, gentleness, and self-control (see Galatians 5:22-23). That means if we choose to act in *opposition* to that, we're not walking in God's love. We can't truly love and be unkind, for example. We can't truly love and be unfaithful. I don't think we even need to get into any of the specific lists of prohibitions we find throughout the Bible, because they simply illustrate all the ways we can be unloving. From worshiping idols to sleeping around to stealing to gossiping, we humans have figured out a nearly infinite number of unloving actions.

And what God is telling us is this: If we want to walk in *his* love, we need to leave all that garbage behind us.

I don't know about you, but what I'm chasing is Love Supreme. Not love-mini or kinda-love. I want the best and the biggest love there is. Not just because I need it either—and the Lord knows how much I need it!—but also because I want to give it away.

I want God's love to save the world.

The Bible explains that *we* love because God first loved us. God showed us *how* by what he *did*. So don't be deceived—true love exists in true actions. Our actions don't *save* us. Jesus saves us. As I like to tell the Crossroads family, we're not saved *by* good works, we're saved *for* good works. That's a subtle but enormous distinction.

Remember Ephesians 2:10? It tells us that *before we were born*, God actually picked out good works for us to do. Insane! God already knows the path of love that he prepared for you to walk on!

We absolutely don't follow that path to earn God's love. Because we can't. And we absolutely don't follow that path to earn our salvation. Because we can't. It's a gift, from start to finish. Grace all the way.

Which might make us ask, *Why does God bother?*

Because of his exceedingly great love.

Because God loves the world—loves us—too much to let us stay the way we are.

Because, as Ephesians 2:10 tells us, God desires that the good things he has planned will be accomplished in the world.

And because God hates evil.

God already knows the hazards and traps on the path he is calling you to walk on, and he wants you to avoid them because he loves you so much, and because he wants you to have the joy of accomplishing the good works—conversations and jobs and prayers and paintings and hugs and travels—he's already prepared for you. For *you*, uniquely!

RIFFING ON THE NEGATIVES

- What are some things that God wants you to stop doing because he loves you?
- How does understanding that love doesn't do certain things change how you view love?

4.5

TIME TO REFLECT

You groped your way through that murk once, but no longer. You're out in the open now. The bright light of Christ makes your way plain. So no more stumbling around. . . . It's a scandal when people waste their lives on things they must do in the darkness where no one will see. Rip the cover off those frauds and see how attractive they look in the light of Christ.

Wake up from your sleep,
Climb out of your coffins;
Christ will show you the light!

EPHESIANS 5:8-9, 12-14

God is calling us to walk with Jesus through the mess. To walk with God's Spirit empowering us. And to walk toward God's perfect, holy future. Toward God's Love Supreme.

We get glimpses of all that goodness in this life. Trouble is, we can't see the full picture. We catch the movie trailer, but we have yet to enjoy the full feature presentation. Still, the teaser, the taste, leaves us wanting more. So we keep walking. And as we walk, we start looking a little more like Jesus. What *we* do starts to look like what *he* would do.

To unpack this, I want to leave you with a word picture that I pray you'll remember two weeks or two decades from now.

It involves darkness and light.

Did you ever learn in school about a mixed metaphor, and how you're not supposed to use one? Like, here's an absolute classic from former Federal Reserve Chair, Ben Bernanke: "[Certain economic data] are guideposts that tell you how we're going to be shifting the mix of our tools as we try to land this ship on a, you know, on a—in a smooth way onto the aircraft carrier."[4] Wow, Ben. Just wow. Hopefully you had a better grasp of monetary policy than language!

But he isn't the only one with mixed metaphors on the brain. Check out what Paul writes in Ephesians 5:11: "Have nothing to do with the fruitless deeds of darkness, but rather expose them" (NIV).

We've got light and darkness, we've got a healthy tree and a withered tree, and we've got what looks like a mixed

---

[4] Josh Boak, "Bernanke, in His Own Words, at 12 News Conferences," Associated Press, December 19, 2013, http://www.ksl.com/?sid=28082948.

metaphor—until we remember that trees need light to make fruit!

Here's where the connection between light and love becomes clear. Think of a couple who own a peach farm.[5] It takes a ridiculous amount of work for them to bring those peaches to market. Like, they could make way more money doing almost anything else. It's a 24-7 responsibility—sometimes backbreaking—to tend that orchard.

So part of why they do it? Not the only reason, but part? Love.

And part of that expression of love is wanting their trees to get the light they need to bear fruit. Our imaginary peach-tree couple *longs* for their trees to get enough light. So their trees can flourish and make the sweetest, juiciest peaches ever! (Anyone want to come over for some fresh peach cobbler?)

Our culture doesn't care much about fruit. Not like God does, anyway. We care about *success*. Remember that classic Jerry Seinfeld description of second place? "Congratulations, you *almost* won. Of all the losers, *you* came in first of that group. You're the number one *loser*!"[6]

So for us it's win at all costs. For God, though, it's all about fruitfulness. Success is limited, because to have a winner, you need a loser. Fruitfulness, though? That can be for the *entire* orchard. For every orchard and tree in the world!

Provided there is enough light.

---

[5] Full disclosure: I could eat about four peaches a day, hence the analogy!
[6] Jerry Seinfeld, *Jerry Seinfeld: I'm Telling You For The Last Time*, 1998.

. . .

The Bible tells us that part of the remedy for the mess of life is to expose the works of darkness.

Let's talk about that word: *expose*. I like to use the example of those high-magnification mirrors that gals sometimes have. Oh wait, I already *did* use that, back on page 28—told you I liked it! When I occasionally get in front of that mirror and flick on that special light, I'm like, "Man, that's *nasty* business!" I seem to have hair follicles on my entire face! I *could* look like Cousin Itt from *The Addams Family*, you know?

Or how about one of those singing competitions, like *The Voice* or *American Idol*? There's always at least one judge who is all *about* picking the nits. There will be this beautiful, heartfelt solo by a well-intentioned and hopeful singer, and then that judge gives this little sniff and says something like, "Well, it *was* a little pitchy . . . so maybe don't quit your day job."

Our job as Christians walking with God is not to nitpick.

Why? Because Jesus said we're not going to be very good at it, considering we have *planks* sticking out of our eyes! (If you're like, "Huh?" then check out Matthew 7.)

We do have a job, however, and that is to expose darkness with light—because the more darkness we expose, the more light there is. Sounds like a lot of work. But the cool thing is that when we walk in God's light, the darkness doesn't stand a chance!

Think about the last time you walked into a dark room

and flicked on the light. Did you hear the light ask the darkness, with an ever-so-polite British accent, "Excuse me, can I have this room for a while? Would you mind moving out? Take your time . . . we can transition gradually!"

Yeah, I didn't think so. The thing about turning on a light is that it dispels the darkness, completely and instantly.

Remember back when we first talked about the remedy for the mess? I think I wrote that remedy a dozen or so times on the pages that followed, because repetition is the greatest teacher, so I *hope* you remember it. (Selfishly, to be honest. I'm being real with you.)

And just as the remedy for the mess is grace and peace, the remedy for darkness is light.

It's that simple.

. . .

But it's also that hard. That messy. Because we can start to believe that it's *our* light. That *we* are responsible for creating it.

But the light inside you? That's not some internal glow you need to get in touch with at a centering workshop—it comes from Jesus! We can't self-generate our own light, no matter how hard we try. We just aren't created that way.

What we *were* created to do with light is to *reflect* it. It's like the sun and the moon. In the book of Genesis, the sun is called the greater light and the moon is called the lesser light. Why? Because the sun *generates* light and the moon *reflects* that light. Like the moon, we weren't created to make light like the sun. Or the Son. Instead, you and I were created to *reflect* God's light, like the moon reflects the sun, out into the darkness, so that others have the light they need to bear fruit and flourish.

"Because of our God's merciful compassion," go the lyrics to one famous song in the Bible, "the Dawn from on high will visit us." Why? Check this: "to shine on those who live in darkness and the shadow of death, to guide our feet into the way of peace" (Luke 1:78-79, HCSB).

So beautiful! So hopeful! You've probably heard the truism, "We are blessed to be a blessing." If the word *blessing* seems too churchy for you, latch on to this idea of light instead. God is the ultimate light in the universe, and *all* other light is a reflection of God's light. Heck, he literally made the stars, as Psalm 33 tells us! And it's because of his great mercy that he shines his perfect light into our lives. The light of hope and love. The light of everything deeply good and truly holy. God's light is the only way we can see clearly enough to walk on the path of peace—and God's light is the only way those of us sitting in darkness have the opportunity to see.

Light is a *big* deal in the Bible. Think about the value of light back then. No electricity, right? So every single lumen of light had to come from the sun, the moon, or a flame. Want to read or sew or walk outside on a moonless night? Better get an oil lamp and find a flame to light it!

Access to light was a basic necessity for survival. Which makes a verse like this stand out in sharper relief: "The people who walk in darkness will see a great light. For those who live in a land of deep darkness, a light will shine" (Isaiah 9:2, NLT).

Or how about one of my favorites, from the first chapter of Colossians: "He has rescued us from the dominion of darkness and brought us into the kingdom of the Son he loves" (verse 13, NIV). Want to take a guess at what characterizes the Son's Kingdom?

The Bible tells us in the book of Revelation: "[It] does not need the sun or the moon to shine on it, for the glory of God gives it light, and the Lamb is its lamp" (21:23, NIV).

Saved from darkness, saved into light.

Saved from ourselves, saved to become our truest selves.

Saved for something bigger than ourselves.

If God's light is shining on you and through you, *even in the mess*, then you *are* "the light of the world. A town built on a hill cannot be hidden. Neither do people light a lamp and put it under a bowl. Instead they put it on its stand, and it gives light to everyone in the house. In the same way, let your light shine before others" (Matthew 5:14-16, NIV).

If we've tasted the Love Supreme, there's no way we can't brag about it!

If the Love Supreme is light, we *have* to reflect it!

RIFFING ON REFLECTION

- What dark areas of your life need to be lit with God's light?
- How do you feel knowing that you don't have to create light, but simply reflect it?

4.6

FILLED TO THE BRIM

Don't drink too much wine. That cheapens your life.
Drink the Spirit of God, huge draughts of him.

EPHESIANS 5:18

I ask him that with both feet planted firmly on love, you'll
be able to take in with all followers of Jesus the extravagant
dimensions of Christ's love. Reach out and experience the breadth!
Test its length! Plumb the depths! Rise to the heights!

EPHESIANS 3:17-18

I can't believe it took me all the way until the end of the book to mention wine—that's pretty much a social faux pas when you're all Italian! But it'll let us take a break from that head-exploding stuff about love and darkness and light. Let's sit down at the Fusco family table and open up a bottle of red.

So in the Bible, Paul uses a street-level picture to make a pretty profound point. He's like, "Hey, stop getting drunk on spirits—and get drunk on *God's* Spirit instead!" (Clever guy, that Paul!)

Here's the reason. When you are intoxicated—don't try this at home . . . and *definitely* don't try this when you're *not* at home—you are in a state we commonly call being "under the influence." People do incredibly dumb things when they're under the influence. Things they wouldn't normally do. Like write on someone's forehead with a Sharpie. Or *allow* their forehead to get written on with a Sharpie. Or even get a tattoo of a Sharpie on their forehead. Or did you ever hear of "beer muscles"? Of course not, you fine upstanding people! Beer muscles are when a little guy has too much to drink and thinks he's a big guy. Since he's under the influence and doesn't have a clue who he really is, he picks a fight with a legitimately big guy—only to get pummeled! He thought he was strong, but his "beer muscles" couldn't really cut it—but I digress!

The point is that alcohol can cut through our normal filters for behavior and lead us to do things we would *never* do otherwise. And with the possible exception of busting a move at a wedding or finally confessing your love for your crush, this is bad idea.[7]

But we can see exactly why Paul chose an analogy that links wine and God's Spirit. Because in the word picture Paul is creating, we should absolutely be "under the influence," but instead of wine—which can make us into idiots—we should be under the influence of God's Spirit, which leads us to act like God.

So the cool and somewhat weird part is this:

Paul is *not* saying: Don't get drunk, and instead be super holy and seriously boring all the time.

Paul *is* saying something closer to: *Do* get drunk, but make sure you're drunk on the right thing, which is God's Spirit, not wine.

---

[7] Actually, the drunken dancing at the wedding is a bad idea too—especially when your friends post it online and it goes viral!

Know what that implies? *God's Spirit changes us in a way that's similar to how alcohol changes us.*[8] And *then* Paul recommends that we be *continually* filled with God's Spirit, on an ongoing basis. Like, "Top me off!"

It's like the time I was in Nepal, visiting my buddy Michael. He picked me up at the airport in Katmandu on a tiny motorbike. Two dudes, with luggage, on a motorbike. Scared yet? I was terrified. As we raced off through the streets and into the mountains, I had plenty of time—as I bear-hugged him in a manly, secure way—to recall Michael learning to drive stick in his Ford Taurus SHO. Once he'd been trying to cross a busy road, only to stall, and as the cross traffic raced toward us, he screamed with his eyes all bugged out, "We're going to die!" We didn't die (obviously), but we did get a good sampling of New Jersey gestures of displeasure.

Anyway, Michael took me to see where he was working, up into one of the villages outside Katmandu. We pulled up to his friend Raptke's home—and whatever you're picturing when I say "home" and "Katmandu" and "mountains," make it smaller and dirtier by about triple—except for the mountains, which you have to multiply by ten. Michael told me that Raptke was dying of TB. So I'd gone from the 747 to fearing for my life on the narrow roads to sitting on the freezing concrete floor of this man, Raptke, who was lying in his bed, covered by a mound of blankets and coughing without reprieve. I was congratulating myself for adjusting so well . . .

---

[8] Go read Acts 2 if you think this is the only time the Bible compares being drunk and being empowered and emboldened by God's Spirit.

But then came the butter tea, served by Raptke's wife.

Look, this won't sound very open minded, but butter tea is terrible. Just the worst. It's basically tea, salt, and yak butter(!) smashed up until it's as thick as motor oil. Also, lukewarm. And did I mention the teapot has visible rust on it?

So we talk, and talk, and talk. Actually, *they* talk, and since I don't speak Nepali, I just sit there. And Michael is an angel. He's flat-out *loving* this family, this man who is about to die, this man who, in the eyes of many, is powerless and nameless and, frankly, worthless. But they are wrong. Raptke matters big time.

So the talk goes on for two hours.

And every time I take a sip of my butter tea—*every single time*—Raptke's wife leans across and tops off my cup. What could I do? I kept drinking, kept saying, "Thank you, thank you"—and finally I prayed, "Lord, will you, like, run this tea out? And please don't let me get sick!"

Michael caught my hints right around the two-hour mark, and graciously asked Raptke's wife to not serve me any more lukewarm butter tea!

But when I think about being topped off by God's Spirit, I can't help but remember that evening in Katmandu. Anytime God's Spirit produces fruit in me—like some kindness toward the person frustrated with the barista who couldn't ever have possibly gotten the most specific and anal drink order in history even remotely correct—then right away I want to ask to be topped off. I want more.

Continually filled with—and under the influence of—God's Spirit. Filled to the brim, constantly.

Because being under God's influence can change everything we do: how we talk and pray and work and walk and love. Everything!

We build each other up instead of tearing each other down. We pray to God when things are terrible and when life seems wonderful. We share the good news with people, honestly and authentically, because we're *living* it. We're grateful instead of bitter. Open to surprises instead of stuck in our ruts. Part of something greater than ourselves. In other words, reflecting the brightness of God's love into dark lives, and a dark world.

Does that sound like the kind of love God calls us toward? Love Supreme? It is!

God loves you so much that he's inviting you to close your eyes and listen to Trane in front of some *seriously* large speakers, or laugh with your family until your stomach hurts, or savor Grandma's favorite dish, and just *revel* in a love beyond what you've ever imagined. It's what you were created for. What you need.

And what the world needs.

RIFFING ON THE OVERFLOW
- What would living under the influence of the Spirit look like?
- How has God loved you extravagantly?

CODA

There's a picture I love on the wall of my office. Fact is, it's a *corner* office—which, now that you know me, you realize is pretty hysterical! I've almost always got music playing, and one wall is taken up with instruments (mostly bass guitars) and amps. The other walls are lined with good books, and there are comfortable couches where we can sit and talk or eat. (Not just donuts, either . . . we go all the way up to cannoli.) And on the wall are two pictures that are important to me—Van Gogh's *Starry Night* and one by Rembrandt. The Rembrandt, painted in the seventeenth century, seems kinda boring at first glance. Not wall-worthy. At first glance it could be any one of thousands of old paintings. A couple of guys dressed in robes, some dark shadows, and some glowing highlights. Not much is happening, really. An older guy is putting his hands on the back of a younger guy, who kneels before him, and that's pretty much it.

Except it's called *The Return of the Prodigal Son*, and once you know that, and once you stare at it awhile, it becomes anything but boring.

The robes start to make more sense—like why the guy who's standing is wearing a thick, rich robe, and why the guy who's kneeling is wearing a threadbare one. The bodies make more sense—the loving, concerned look of the father and the hunched shoulders of a son weathered by his own decisions.

The prodigal son has returned home, and the father has chosen to embrace him rather than reject him. I like to call that "the sacred embrace." In Rembrandt's painting, the hands of the father demand our attention. One is powerful, muscled and strong, as if ready to lift the son up or fight to protect him. One is tender and soft, as if ready to hold and comfort the son. They are the hands of God—God's sacred embrace holding us, and keeping us.

You know, I think John Coltrane would have loved that picture. For all I know, he did!

See, in a lot of ways Trane *was* a prodigal son. A lot of times we think *prodigal* means something like "bad" or "rebellious" because we know what happens in the parable: The son runs away and does a whole slew of dirty deeds, all with his dad's cash! Coltrane had that in his story, with a background of addiction issues. But *prodigal* also has another meaning. We hear it in words like *prodigious* and *prodigy*, and it means lavish and extravagant.

Which is also a lot like Trane. Dude was one of the most gifted—most prodigious—artists of the century, period. One of America's most gifted citizens. But genius and fame didn't shield him from the messiness of life. Quite the opposite.

An African American thrust into the public spotlight the decade *before* the civil rights movement took hold.

An intensely shy man gifted beyond measure as a public performer.

A man wired up for addiction who beat heroin and alcohol, only to become addicted to music, driving himself to practice all night long—at least until his untimely death from cancer at the tender age of forty.

Raised a Christian, married to a Muslim, seeking truth in Eastern spirituality.

And what was the result of that incredible amount of messiness?

One of the greatest, most profound, most spiritual works of art ever. *A Love Supreme*. The album that blew open my and Ilya's minds and hearts that night we listened to it back in college. An album that fused, for the first time, elements from all of Coltrane's diverse styles. There was hard bop, with its quick tempos and frequent chord changes. There was modal jazz, focusing its exploration of possibility on a single tonal center. And there was free jazz, in which he and his band improvised music without the structure of chords or even timing. It was recorded in a *single day*—December 9, 1964— and released in February 1965. Four harmonious movements. Acknowledgement. Resolution. Pursuance. Psalm.

Listen to how Trane phrased it in the liner notes:

> *God will wash away all our tears . . .*
> *He always has . . .*
> *He always will.*
> *Seek Him every day. In all ways seek God every day.*
> *Let us sing all songs to God*
> *To whom all praise is due . . . praise God.*

Not just a musical landscape changed. A *life* changed. A prodigal son running back to his Father. And maybe that's why I love that album so much: because when Trane finally "came home" like the boy in the parable told by Jesus, he found his Father—and more.

He found himself. His *truest* self—the one God knit together in the womb, the one God created to do good works, even before Trane was born.

I've got a little theory, by the way, that I want to share. More of a hope, really, or something I suspect. What if human culture doesn't disappear at the end of time, when Jesus makes a new heaven and a new earth and we get to live with God forever? We sometimes talk like *culture* is a bad word, but God created us, way back in the Garden, to work. To create and cultivate and produce. And even after we started sinning our brains out, God saved us *unto* good works. And gifted us with intuition and creativity and passion and intelligence. Know what an example of a "good work" is? Healing the sick and clothing the naked. Know what else? Jackson Pollock's painting *Convergence*. The compositions of Anthony Braxton or John Zorn. The directing of Darren Aronofsky. The famous cut fastball from Mariano Rivera to end the game. Frank Lloyd Wright's "Fallingwater" home. (Please insert your own examples here!)

Which is why reading Revelation 21:24 gives me a thrill, of hope: "And the kings of the earth will bring their splendor into [the heavenly city]" (NIV). We might be listening to *A Love Supreme* in eternity!

John Coltrane had a PhD in messiness, yet he said this: *"May we never forget that in the sunshine of our lives, through the storm and after the rain—it is all with God—in all ways and forever."*

I like that because it's as good a summary of the messiness of life as I've heard. Sunshine, storm, and the clearing away of clouds. Repeat *ad infinitum*.

Except not forever, not really, but only repeat until the end of our lives. Of this life. Because the only things that will be repeated forever are the things of God, the things we do in God and for God, the things God brings to fruition in his present and future and forever Kingdom. When the clouds clear away for the final time, my friends, they will not return. Not in a thousand years. Not ever.

See, Coltrane is us. The prodigal son is us. Every wayward son and wayward daughter is us.

Beaten up, used up, at the end of a dead-end road.

But coming home.

Despite everything, despite everyone, coming home.

Walking down that long, dusty road, retracing our steps, scarcely daring to hope. Unwilling to expect anything good, *because we are not good*. We know ourselves all too well, and the prognosis is death. We are being honest about who and how we are! The best we can hope for upon returning home? A slave's welcome. Enough food to keep us alive while we work ourselves to death, trying to pay our debt. Life is messy, after all. Messy through and through, and like ink added to water. We cannot even dream of undoing it.

Except.

Except while you are still a long way off—kicking up dust along the road of despair—while you are still an insignificant speck in the distance, God comes running. Sprinting! Can you imagine? Do you dare? That the One who knows the name of every star, all one hundred octillion of them, knows *you* better than you know yourself!

And instead of spitting out that inky water that is your life, he makes it clean. "This means that anyone who belongs to Christ has become a new person. The old life is gone; a new life has begun!" (2 Corinthians 5:17, NLT).

Just like that. And forever.

The prodigal son never got a chance to speak the complete apology he'd composed on his journey. He couldn't because he was already clutched tight to the chest of his Father, weeping with joy. He was in God's sacred embrace, and God will never let go!

Remember, God doesn't make bad people good. That's pocket change. Low-hanging fruit. God thinks bigger—so big it's impossible.

God makes dead people alive.

What did the father have the right to say to his prodigal son? The same thing the son said earlier to his father: you're *dead* to me. And here's what the running father—what God—actually said: "This son of mine was dead and is alive again; he was lost and is found" (Luke 15:24, NIV).

Dead / Alive.

Lost / Found.

And always, *always* Jesus.

That's light. All the light we need. The light shines in the darkness—*especially in the darkness of our lives*—and the darkness cannot overcome it!

That's love. The perfect love of God. A love that cannot be denied or changed. A love that changes everything. Love Supreme.

Life is messy. Jesus is real. That's the good news written on the first page of the first chapter of the rest of your life.

Grace and peace to you.

Go and walk with Jesus into your beautiful mess.

RIFFING ON COMING HOME

- In what ways have you been that prodigal?
- Where can you see Jesus' beauty and love shining in the midst of your mess?